Soul Space

Creating Places and Lives that Make a Difference

Linda Lawrence Hunt

Tasora

Minneapolis, Minnesota

TO ORDER: To order books, and for further information on the Krista Foundation for Global Citizenship, please visit www.kristafoundation.org. Book profits support the Krista Foundation.

Soul Space: Creating Places and Lives that Make a Difference

ISBN 978-1-934690-98-7

Tasora

Tasora Books
5120 Cedar Lake Road S
Minneapolis, MN 55416
(952) 345-4488

Distributed by Itasca Books
Printed in the U.S.A.

For Jim,

whose vision, delight in nature,

and faithful tending of the land

make creating a place of

welcome and beauty

a joy to share.

Prior to construction, guests gathered for a time of a "Blessing of the Hearth" and joined in seven specific blessing prayers. In the next seventeen years, comments in guest books illuminate how experiences in the Hearth and gardens give meaning to these early blessings. Their comments are featured throughout Soul Space.

Contents

Prologue

The Krista Foundation for Global Citizenship and the Hearth and gardens began in tragedy on a remote mountain in Bolivia. Our daughter, Krista Hunt Ausland, was six months into serving a three-year volunteer assignment in Bañado de la Cruz with her husband Aaron when she died in a traumatic bus accident. The stories in *Soul Space* illuminate the surprise discovery of the unfolding blessings within our sorrow of places that invite others into a circle of belonging and nature's beauty. Places that can make a difference in our stress-filled contemporary life.

Krista and Aaron's dream was to eventually enter graduate school for careers in international affairs. When telling our families why they needed to move over 7000 miles from their Washington State home, they explained, "As Americans, we need to listen first. Otherwise, how can we engage in creating public policies that impact citizens in other nations?"

So after college graduation from the University of Puget Sound, they spent two summers driving tour buses in Alaska to pay off student debts. Then Krista taught biology and math for a year in a difficult urban high school in Tacoma, Washington. After exploring volunteer opportunities, they applied to serve with the Mennonite Central Committee, commonly known as MCC. They felt drawn to this organization's long and thoughtful history serving the poor and its skillful efforts in peacemaking around the world. Though Krista grew up in the Presbyterian tradition, they both appreciated MCC's philosophy that included a "ministry of presence" by living among the people. Krista's desire, expressed in her application, included her hope to "show God's love through actions."

LEFT Aaron and Krista on graduation day at the University of Puget Sound.

RIGHT Traditional methods for a farmer tilling fields near Bañado de la Cruz.

ABOVE Aaron and Krista by their Bolivian one-room adobe home that also housed a second room for the community farmer's cooperative.

ABOVE Krista loved building friendships and discussing nutrition while cooking with the Women's Cooperative on her front porch.

Their placement was in Bañado de la Cruz, a very isolated valley with 50 farm families who lived great distances from one another along the Comarapa River.

Krista and Aaron's one-room adobe home and front porch offered a welcoming place for the women's cooperative and the men's agricultural room that connected to the side of the house.

On first sight of their living quarters, Krista felt distressed. "We romanticize adobe homes in America," she wrote. "In fact, I live in a house made of straw and mud that looks like it will disintegrate in the first rainfall. It looks like crap."

But within a short time she came to love her new abode. The Quaker song "A Gift to be Simple" tells of living in the "valley of love and delight," and she began to experience a taste of this as she wrote,

I love it here and am increasingly content and happy with my new home. It gives me a peace which seeps into my soul. I love the peaceful view from our porch and the fact that there are more pigs and goats than cars on our quiet road. I love taking hikes, I love getting strong carrying water, and I love what being here does for our marriage.

ABOVE Common mode of preparing meals outdoors for farm women in Bañado.

RIGHT With few toys, local boys find creative ways for play.

Besides working in the local women's cooperative, she began developing children's literacy programs through libraries in two larger towns. This required walking or riding her motorcycle hours away. Their first major local project included hosting a church youth group that came from Canada to help Bañado's Bolivian families build dry latrines. Prior to this, no bathrooms existed, so people also lacked privacy for personal needs.

Without electricity, and with water needing to be hauled from distant springs or the river, Krista and Aaron managed to create a loving, welcoming home. She relished the simple pleasures of becoming a part of her new community, especially as women from the cooperative gathered weekly on her porch. Many were far younger than Krista and most had children in tow. She wrote,

> Monday afternoon was the women's group reunion. "We processed their future plans and then cooked our stuffed green peppers. The cooking was beautiful if it could be such a thing. We sat around cutting onions, spices, and cooking everything on the open fire. The women shifted tasks as babies cried, or children needed attention.

Her friendly puppy Choclo also hung out on the porch. Because dogs often experienced abuse or neglect in the countryside, the women found themselves fascinated by Krista's tenderness to Choclo, and how that seemed to shape his happy personality.

On the evening of May 20, 1998, Krista and Aaron boarded a bus in Comarapa, the nearest town. They planned to attend a conference retreat eight hours away in Santa Cruz, the vibrant capital city of the eastern region of Bolivia. For a while, they dozed peacefully with 35 other passengers while their puppy slept on their laps.

Near midnight, the speeding bus driver lost control, careening over a high mountain cliff, and plunging to the bottom of a deep ravine. Aaron and Choclo were thrown out at the top. Though injured, Aaron scrambled down the mountainside in the pitch dark, touching all of the bodies as he tried to find Krista. Finally he discovered her near the bus, which was tipping precariously over his beloved wife's body. In that moment, his dreams of their life together shattered suddenly like the thousand shards of glass littering the mountainside.

ABOVE Aaron designed and placed a permanent marker on the hillside highway where Krista died.

During the following year, our family entered into profound sorrow with Aaron. Our primary comfort came from the abundant love of friends and family. They lamented with us over the loss of the inspiring love that Krista's too brief life gave so many.

But Jim and I also received dire warnings from people. Many people said that after the death of a child "everything changes," and that marriages often end since couples are unable to sustain the burdens of grief.

This caused us to talk together about how we now wanted to live. I was especially influenced by the teachings of Viktor Frankl, author of *Man's Search for Meaning*. We taught this insightful book in our Core 150 classes at Whitworth University where I was a professor. An Austrian psychiatrist, Frankl survived imprisonment in horrific Nazi concentration camps, including Auschwitz. When he discovered that some prisoners could transcend the terror and daily evil they endured, he became fascinated with their interior lives. He observed that these men lived with eloquent courage, compassion, and dignity. They even offered comfort and gave their last scrap of bread to others. In contrast, those who shut down in hopelessness often died in days.

Convinced that "human choice" made the pivotal difference, he believed that though one cannot always choose the experiences life gives, "we do have the power to choose one's attitude, to choose one's way in any given circumstances."

An immediate choice facing us was whether Jim, a history professor, would continue his 25 years of sharing faculty leadership in Whitworth University's five-month Central American Study-Service trips. This would mean re-entering a world where taking public transportation always created risk. However, Jim believed the learning provided for young adults was unparalleled. He found these trips so satisfying for faculty and students that our daughters Susan and Krista had both left their universities for a semester to join Whitworth's distinctive program. Although concerned, neither of us believed Jim needed to let go of his involvement. Once again, he said "yes."

One of our family customs when traveling abroad or in large American cities is to find a cathedral or church where we can light candles to pray for our children. The spring after Krista's death, when Jim arrived with 25 students in San Salvador, he planned to light candles for her, our son Jefferson, and our daughter Susan in the large cathedral.

However, in the midst of a renovation, he found no candles in the cathedral. On the

BELOW Jim lighting candles for our children and their families, a custom throughout our travels.

following day, he took students to La Divina Providencia to introduce them to this small sacred space. It was here in 1980 that Archbishop Óscar Romero was assassinated just as he lifted the chalice in celebration of Mass. Jim once shared this place with Krista and these searing memories broke his heart. After lighting candles, all his pent up sorrow released into unrelenting tears.

Isabel Allende, the Chilean writer who described the lingering loss of her daughter in *Paula*, wrote us a letter after reading an essay I wrote called "A Terrible Beauty." This described the journey of our loss, which paralleled hers, since both daughters were spirited, beautiful brunette 25-year-olds, who were married and compassionately involved in inner city concerns. In a hand-crafted card, she wrote, "I hope someday you'll have sweet dreams of Krista."

"I'd never been able to dream of her," recalls Jim. "The pain was just so unbearable and blocked. But that night, after my emotional release, I had my first sweet dream where she was a young child coming to me. The next day I called Linda and said, 'We've got to do something besides cry to remember our daughter.'"

My own path to healing often led me to finding solace in the garden. Jim used to tease me that it would be far easier on our finances if I went to a grief therapist. During the weeks Jim was traveling in a risky land, I started preparing the soil after designing an expanded bed for more roses and Chinese Tree peonies. Unknown to him, I also had been pondering the possible ways we could honor Krista's memory. These stirrings in our hearts and minds, while thousands of miles apart, gave birth to the Krista Foundation for Global

ABOVE June treasures of Chinese tree peonies, lilacs, and purple columbine.

Citizenship community, and eventually the illuminating beauty of the Hearth and gardens.

But when we began, we knew little of what lay ahead. We only knew that the deep wellspring of fierce love and sorrow burdening our hearts needed a healthy means of expression. We wanted to share the beauty of her vision, interrupted far too soon. But how? This is the unfolding story of what emerged. ✑

ABOVE Krista near her remote home by the Rio Comarapa, Bolivia. Families lived in farms scattered along the river rather than in a village, often located at significant distances from one another.

Chapter I

A Treasure of a Different Sort

"Faith is taking the first step
when you can't see
the whole staircase."

~Martin Luther King, Jr.

CLOCKWISE FROM TOP LEFT Children learn early how to help parents plant seeds. The only tiny storefront in the community—every week, except when the river floods, farmers walk or join a pickup truck to carry their crops to the Comarapa market, over three miles away. After a few bruise-inducing crashes, Krista learned to ride a motorcycle, her and Aaron's only transportation between distant towns and villages where they served.

I t was the towering Illimani mountain that drew my husband, Jim, and me to the window as our airplane lifted off from La Paz on the last leg of a 6000 mile journey to Santa Cruz, Bolivia. But our thoughts ranged to another Bolivian mountain, where in the past May our daughter Krista lay dying. It was August when we joined our son-in-law, Aaron, in a visit to the land of our daughter's last days. A generous invitation from MCC offered the opportunity to return with him to meet all who knew and loved her. We also wanted to be alongside him as he grieved closing the first real home he and Krista had shared. When we arrived in Santa Cruz, we each felt the stinging reality of the poet Mark Doty's words, "How could I ever prepare for an absence the size of you?"

For nine hours, we bounced along the rutted highways in an old pickup truck to arrive at the Bañado de la Cruz river valley. The community had no village center, but included subsistence farms spread along the river.

MCC had given Aaron and Krista motorcycles, so she'd needed to learn to negotiate narrow rocky mountain trails where many spills left her badly bruised. "As we met families, I felt I needed to explain the cause of my bruises so they didn't assume they came from Aaron," she wrote. "It's sad that women's bruises here are often caused by domestic violence."

When women in the local cooperative heard Aaron was returning with us, they cooked a generous country feast of chicken, rice, and lettuce and tomato salad. Gathered together around the table in the one-room school, these normally very reserved young women spoke their own stories of sorrow at losing Krista's friendship. Several of the mothers, with babies slung on their backs, looked

ABOVE Throughout Krista's times in Central America, she gravitated to knowing and caring for children.

much younger than Krista. They even shared their nightly dreams of her.

The women lived harsh and difficult lives, beginning in childhood. They worked daily without the benefits of potable water, electricity, health care, sanitation, and literacy, because so little schooling was provided.

But as Krista came to know the women's stories, she respected their resilience and strength. She marveled at her 50-year-old neighbor Dionisea, a mother of 12 and local herbalist. She still worked the fields, and she walked six miles round-trip to the nearest town to get groceries. "Krista called her the Tina Turner of the community," Aaron said, "because she had such strong legs." It was these women who initiated the project to build dry latrines for their families and hosted and fed the Canadian church students who came to help.

They took turns offering words that described Krista. "Alegria!" said Dionisea, and the women murmured their assent to this Spanish word for joy. Others mentioned she was "a good friend," "helpful," "a hard worker," "very funny," "a lover of children and animals," and "so encouraging." It was humbling to hear how much genuine affection and respect can grow between women from such diverse worlds, a power that allowed women to bridge the boundaries of culture.

The next day, we visited Saipina, where city leaders hosted us for the opening celebration of a new library. They named it in Krista's honor for her efforts there.

After we returned home to Spokane with these many treasured memories, we found ourselves pondering, "How do we live with this crevasse in our lives? How do we weave her memory into the fabric of our family forever?" By the summer of 1999, when Jim returned from taking students from Whitworth down to Central America again, we felt ready to create a legacy in her memory.

But what? We sought wisdom from others who loved Krista and knew of her vision, trying to discern what best to create. One pivotal perspective came from Sharon Daloz Parks, a professor and researcher at Harvard Divinity School. A friend since we'd met while volunteering with college ministry at University Presbyterian Church in Seattle, we had also worked together at Whitworth University when she'd served as Associate Chaplain

ABOVE Their beloved neighbor, Dionisea, an herbalist and mother of 12, introduced Aaron and Krista to local medicinal herbs that help heal minor illnesses. **BELOW** The town of Saipina named their new library in honor of Krista's work with local children's literacy and held a celebration during our visit there.

there. She had lived in our rental cottage next door and, most importantly, she'd become Krista and Susan's godmother.

Parks's research on faith development led to her book *Big Questions, Worthy Dreams: Mentoring Emerging Adults in Their Search for Meaning, Purpose, and Faith*. This significant contribution offers insight for mentors during these critical years.

One of her premises is that young people often receive significant support during their school years, even through college if they attend. But in contemporary American society, when they enter their pivotal twenties, she believed they "often enter a kind of abyss with very little support." No longer marrying early or choosing immediate careers, especially amidst economic downturns, their twenties are still often the decade when they make major life-shaping decisions. Their choices, such as eventual career paths, commitments to relationships, and their emerging morality, faith, and worldview often are determined then. She believed young adults need "networks of belonging," communities of "both comfort and challenge" during these years.

Jim and I also knew many other young adults who shared a similar vision to Krista's and planned a volunteer commitment after college. Some joined large government-sponsored service organizations, such as the Peace Corps or AmeriCorps. Others chose smaller faith-based young adult organizations from a variety of Protestant and Catholic traditions, such as Jesuit Volunteer Corps, Lutheran Volunteer Corps, PCUSA Young Adult Volunteers, MCC Salt, or L'Arche. We began to see how creating an intergenerational community of support for young adults with a service ethic connected genuinely to Krista's life and vision.

So that summer, Jim and I pored through the hundreds of condolence letters that we had kept. As university professors at a small Presbyterian liberal arts college, we lacked any extra funds. So

ABOVE Krista with her biology students at Wilson High School in Tacoma, Wa., where she developed an innovative peer tutoring program for students.

we wrote a letter to those who grieved her death inviting them to help initiate the Krista Foundation for Global Citizenship.

We shared our initial hopes and dreams to create a cohort class each year of young adults, like Krista, who planned to volunteer with an agency for a year or more of service. Modeled loosely after the Fulbright Scholar program, we planned for university, civic, and church leaders to nominate potential Krista Colleagues. We looked for those who demonstrated a spirit of service, not just exceptional academic excellence.

Recognizing the need to narrow our selection process, we chose to initially focus on young adults volunteering in Krista's three primary areas of concern. After graduation, she'd taught biology and math at Wilson High School where she had initiated an innovative peer-tutoring program. So we included one category for Colleagues volunteering in the United States challenging urban centers.

We added Developing Nations as a second category. That emerged from Krista's many

ABOVE Evelyn Christensen, Krista's grandmother, gave the first generous gift to begin the Krista Foundation.

Believing in the importance for young adults to develop ongoing skills, we added a $1000 Service-Leadership grant. This idea came from Krista's situation. She wanted eventually to attend graduate school, but she lacked advanced statistical work. From her Alaska savings, she drew out $500 for an online course to complete while serving in Bolivia. But we recognized many young adults lack such savings, and volunteer stipends leave no financial reserve.

Convinced that "lone-ranger volunteerism" seldom enriches a community, one stipulation was that all Krista Colleagues serve with an existing agency that offers opportunities in hands-on service. Organizations utilizing young adults for evangelism as their primary goal are not included since many churches already support these. As a designated 501c3 educational foundation with the IRS, we planned to provide service-ethics preparation before service, support during service, and most-importantly, support for three more years after Colleagues complete their service assignments.

Whitworth University learned the importance of this post-service support after seeing how students in their five-month Central America study-service trip had such powerful and life-changing experiences. However, when students were not prepared enough beforehand or debriefed significantly afterwards, faculty also saw that such experiences sometimes led students to unsettling dysfunction, and even to dropping out of school.

Returning to America's consumer-oriented society left some students feeling isolated and alienated. So the Latin American faculty teams began integrating significant follow-up after students returned. This proved invaluable for positive post-service growth. Our awareness of the importance of such support greatly influenced the design of our initial programs.

experiences in Central America, including a transformative summer as a 16-year-old exchange student in Guatemala. Our third category invites nominees engaged in Environmental Projects. This recognized her sustaining interest since elementary school in science and the environment, and her holistic belief in God's love for all creation.

We also sought young adults motivated for service as a way of living out their Christian faith through tangible actions. The cohort group of Krista Colleagues each year would be "twenty-somethings," ages 20 to 29, and would also have some loose connection to the Northwest. They might grow up in the East but be volunteering in Portland, Oregon, or grow up in the West and go to college or work elsewhere.

ABOVE Tom and Valerie Norwood volunteered in Kenya with the PCUSA, Presbyterian Church Young Adult Year in Mission.

ABOVE Valerie Norwood, a Krista Colleague in the Charter Class, now serves as Executive Director of the Krista Foundation.

Encouraging a spirit of joy in service, not treating it as some grim duty, became another central focus, shaped by Krista and Aaron's own approach. A fellow MCC volunteer, Jeremy Funk, captured this spirit in his poem *Joy Dance*, which he wrote the night she died. When Aaron and Krista moved to Bolivia, they spent the first few months in language school in Santa Cruz where MCC drew volunteers together at their headquarters. While there, they cooked with Jeremy and became good friends with him. An English major and poet, he lives with the daily challenges of cerebral palsy that hinder his movement.

One evening they joined in a quinceañera celebration for a staff member's 15-year-old daughter. During this traditional Bolivian celebration signifying the transition from girlhood to becoming a young woman, Krista invited Jeremy onto the dance floor. This was a new experience

for him as they gently shuffled to the music.

When word came in from the countryside that Krista had been killed, his anguish kept him up all night writing *Joy Dance*. This poem has become a symbol of how we hope young adults will embrace service, and we incorporated this concept as one of the principles of service leadership in our program.

In the fall of 1999, our talented Board of Directors welcomed our first cohort class of Krista Colleagues. Several of the nine initial Colleagues were friends of Krista's who planned to serve as she did. "Needless to say, we were entering our assignments with our eyes open to the reality of dangers in service," said Krista's close friend Valerie Norwood, now Executive Director of the foundation. She and her husband Tom were just embarking on an assignment outside Nairobi, Kenya with the Young Adult Presbyterian Year in Mission when she became a Colleague.

Aaron joined part of this initial class since he planned to return to Bolivia to continue his and Krista's initial commitment. However, he requested to live in Santa Cruz to assist with microfinancing projects. He knew if he lived alone in the remote village, the isolation and memories would intensify his profound grief.

Generous funds came in, mostly small amounts, but also a $25,000 gift from Kevin and Joan Brown, a young couple who volunteered in their twenties for a year with Habitat for Humanity in Americus, Georgia. "That year changed us, so we fully understand why this support makes sense," Joan wrote. "We are bringing all we learned that year into our work as teachers and engineers." Kevin had received a windfall from the sale of a start-up computer business and they wanted to tithe their profit to us. Krista's grandmother, Evelyn Christensen, also gave $25,000 to help us begin. She loved Krista dearly and knew the pain of losing her only son Larry, my brother, at almost the same age. A sorrow that never ended.

We received another important gift in a letter to Aaron, which he read to us on our way to the airport for our Bolivia trip. Lynn Caruso, a poet and lifelong family friend, described fellow poet Mark Doty's metaphor:

> Doty describes ancient Japanese ceramic cups. These cups were once the property of some holy monk, one of the few possessions he permitted himself to keep. Centuries later, the cup was dropped and broken, but even in this condition it was too beautiful to simply destroy. So it was repaired, not with glue, which wouldn't hold for centuries to come, but with a thin seam of gold solder repairing the break in what could never truly be repaired perfectly. The gold solder added a beauty to the cup, making part of it quite visible.

> The metaphor offers the possibility to honor the part of oneself that's irreparable.

ABOVE On Krista's birthday, Jim surprised me with this stone frame laced with gold solder surrounding her smiling photograph. A joy forever!

ABOVE Kinsugi bowl created by Morty Bachar, Lakeside Pottery Studio

> To fill the crack with gold means to give the break prominence, to let it shine. Wearing its history, the old cup with its gilt scars becomes, I imagine, a treasure of another sort, whole in its own fragmentation, more deeply itself, veined with the evidence of time.

JOY DANCE
I CELEBRATE YOUR JOY

JEREMY FUNK

The night I met you we saw gauchos
stomp black boots, wave white sombreros,
twirl rings of fire. Laughter danced
in your eyes and your face flickered
in the half-dark as we tried to talk
above charangos, quenas, and drums.

Already in the throaty throb
of that music I knew your joy.
I learned more about the dance
of your life when you begged Aaron
to learn folk-steps on the cancha after cards.

Later in the green elegance of a quince party,
Aaron escorted you to the turf to dance.
A love-dance. Lively from love,
drinking juicy band music,
You asked me to join in a joy-dance.

You held both my hands and I shuffled
on the lawn, feet heavy as stones.
Now in darkness the weight of marble
my stomach churns from too many tears
and I hear only my heartbeat; a tricky rhythm,
like Aaron's drumming on talent night.

The table is cool to my face warm
    from weeping.
Against the heavy harmony of silence

I sing to prolong music quiet too soon:
your dance, the dance of your life.
How to hear these fragments of song,
these jagged melodies? They barb us,
gouge us, gore us. They chill us,
these dances frozen in the heart of sway.

If I cannot prolong your dance, I will
proclaim it. I will proclaim your dance
to God and to the world. I will celebrate
a dance of flavors: tomatoes, oregano, basil
when you cooked pasta with me in the kitchen.

I will remember how you made me laugh,
how laughter swam in your voice.
I won't forget the way you giggled and tugged
at Aaron's questions across the supper table,
both wishing for a cup of Starbucks coffee.

Paging through my journal and listening
To the night, I hear hens in
recitative. Dogs whimper.
Leaves flap, or angel wings.

Treetops bend and sway, like my spirit
this night: bowing yet dancing.
And in the breeze that lures these trees
    to praise
I almost hear you singing hallelujah.

Chapter II

The Hearth Is Born

*"Everyone needs beauty
as well as bread,
places to play in and pray in,
where nature may heal
and give strength
to body and soul alike."*

~John Muir, Founder of the Sierra Club

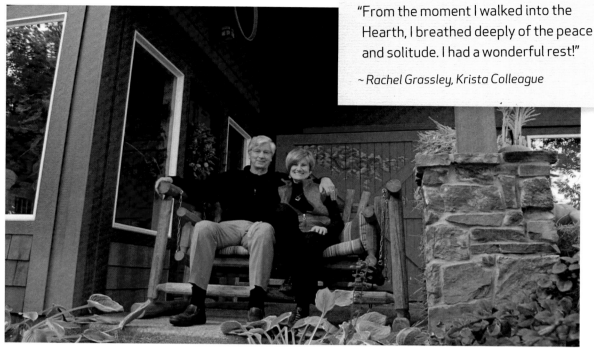

"From the moment I walked into the Hearth, I breathed deeply of the peace and solitude. I had a wonderful rest!"

~ *Rachel Grassley, Krista Colleague*

ABOVE Jim and Linda Hunt relaxing by the Hearth entry.

In 2000, after we gathered the second year Krista Colleague cohort class to meet in the back yard of our home, it became apparent how helpful it could be to create a centering place for the foundation. Twenty-somethings are often uprooted. While they are living in new communities where work can be found, their parents may change homes or at least reclaim their bedrooms from childhood. If they're volunteering, some agency assignments bring them to an unfamiliar city or even another country.

We thought if we could root the idea of the Krista Foundation in a tangible place that encourages community, this might offer a further sense of support. So, in 2001, we tore down a dilapidated barn above our home, where our three children once raised pygmy goats, chickens, rabbits, and a Palomino horse.

After the barn's removal, we invited friends to join us for a "Blessing of the Hearth," and we set up tiki lamps throughout the footprint of where the Hearth would be built. We especially cared about blessing the artisans, unknown persons who would be working to create a place of beauty. Whether the architect and builder, framers, stonemasons for the fireplace, painters, or furniture makers, we wanted anyone engaged in creating this space to find joy and inspired skill in their contribution.

We composed a reading for our guests to share with us, sending our prayers together that this might become a place of inspiration and peace for many. So that evening we walked together along where the Hearth would rise, stopping near all corners to share a common prayer.

OPPOSITE (top left) Remnants of the old barn being torn down to build the Hearth. **(top right)** The stone staircase winds up from the Asian garden and patio to the Hearth.

Blessing of the Hearth

FOR COMFORT:

When Your people need comfort, may the peace in this soul space and these gardens offer healing and hope, giving visual assurance that God hears the brokenhearted, offering the Biblical promise that You will turn our mourning into dancing and clothe us with joy, so that we will give thanks to You forever.

Community: Bless the Hearth, O Lord we pray.

FOR COUNSEL:

During times when decisions confront us, may this soul space provide moments of quietude and contemplation, giving us a chance to hear ourselves and receive Your guidance, experiencing the Psalmist's wisdom:

> I bless the Lord who gives me counsel; in the night also my heart instructs me. I keep the Lord always before me...Therefore my heart is glad, and my soul rejoices, my body also rests secure. You show me the path of life.

As we find insight by listening to ourselves and You, may we also grow in learning to listen to others, with attentiveness and welcome.

Community: Bless the Hearth, O Lord we pray.

FOR CHALLENGES:

When groups gather around the hearth for a common purpose, illuminate their vision to see the world with Your eyes for our homes, cities, and global communities. During times when the needs of this world can overwhelm, help us to remember the United Nations' Secretary-General Dag Hammarskjöld's words, "In our era, the road to holiness necessarily passes through the world of action." Sharpen our awareness of those particular areas where the boldness and energy of our active commitments, creativity, and passions can create a better world for others.

Community: Bless the Hearth, O Lord we pray.

FOR CONVERSATION:

When friends share this communal space, may it help forge the foundation of friendships, drawing us into the companionship our Creator desires. Lift forth our best selves around the feasting of table, fun, art, music, and natural wonder. May Your spirit abound in conversations around the pond and waterfall, on patios, in the Great Room, the library, and wanderings in the garden. Thank you for the gifts of intellect and heart that you generously give. May this Hearth become one place of belonging for people from around the world and for people serving around the world.

Community: Bless the Hearth, O Lord we pray.

FOR CONTEMPLATION:

May this Hearth and these gardens compel our commitment to stewardship of the earth, so wisely expressed in the 12th century by Hildegard of Bingen, and later by 20th century poet Archibald MacLeish after he saw films of our planet taken from space.

Glance at the sun. See the moon and the stars.
Gaze at the beauty of earth's greenings.
Now, think.
What delight God gives to humankind
With all these things...
All nature is at the disposal of humankind.
We are to work with it. For
Without it, we cannot survive.

~HILDEGARD

To see the earth as it truly is, small and blue and beautiful in that eternal silence where it floats, is to see ourselves as riders on the earth together, brothers on that bright loveliness in the eternal cold—brothers who know now they are truly brothers.

~MACLEISH

Community: *Bless the Hearth, O Lord we pray.*

FOR COMPASSION:

May renewal at the Hearth enliven our spirit of compassion, growing as global citizens. Encourage our desire to practice the spirit of loving-kindness in our daily lives: to ourselves, our families, our communities, all creatures great and small, and our planet home.

Community: *Bless the Hearth, O Lord we pray.*

FOR CONFIDENCE AND COURAGE:

Let us leave the Hearth infused with Thy Spirit, confident in Jesus's promise that we are not alone. In a world that hungers for peace, use the gatherings in this space to help us walk humbly on this earth, but with abundant belief that we are to "Be strong and of good courage, for I will be with You."

Community: *These are bold prayers, O God, but Your ways are higher than our ways, and Your thoughts higher than our thoughts. We entrust these prayers to you. Bless this Hearth, O Lord we pray!*

"Each time I sit on the edge of the pond, that mysterious vine-covered blue door captures my attention, as if it were a passageway to another land. Perhaps a portal to Narnia. And I am peaceful. This mood describes the garden. A peace garden. Created for a beautiful daughter and friend. Beauty out of immense pain and loss. Truly, we can declare that God is good."

~ Jack Brace, Krista Colleague and friend of Krista's in college

ABOVE Around age 10, Krista and childhood friend Julienne Gage dipped into a can of paint and "decorated" the original barn door with their handprints. Artist Kathy Peterson added the daisies, trees, and quail. The traditional painted cart is from Sarchi, Costa Rica.

"The beauty here is everywhere.
It lives and breathes and fills
our hearts. We want to live with
awakened hearts!"

~ *Cheryl, on a Woman's Retreat*

That evening someone mentioned, "I know of a family who put prayers in their home's foundation. You might think about this." Liking this suggestion, the next day we sent an email to Krista Colleagues serving around the world. Many sent in their favorite prayers from spiritual influencers like Mother Teresa or Bishop Tutu. Some sent very personal ones. We printed these off, wadded them up and placed them throughout the Hearth's foundation.

The day the workers came to pour the foundation, they immediately asked, "What are these wads of paper?" Thankfully, they assured us that keeping them wouldn't compromise the quality of their task. Several weeks later, while the Hearth was still in the incomplete stages of construction and the stonemasons were building the fireplace, the workers called our builder. "Could we bring our wives over and show them what we're helping create? This place has such a spirit of peace." We felt deeply honored that they felt this peace so early in the construction.

Since Jim and I didn't actually have funds to build the Hearth, and we didn't believe funds should be drawn from donations to the Krista Foundation, we refinanced our home mortgage. Then we could move ahead. Codes required the Hearth to be situated on the footprint of the barn, but they allowed one extended wing.

During demolition, we salvaged the original barn door. In a day of childhood mischief, Krista and her childhood friend Julienne Gage dipped their hands into cans of white paint and left their handprints throughout the stables and on the door. It actually charmed us when they were 10-year-olds, and of course, it especially charms us now. So we saved this large sliding door to accent the exterior. An artist friend, Kathy Peterson, painted scenes from our garden to include a field of daisies, Krista's favorite flower, and the California quail that roam our land.

On the main floor, guests are welcomed through a slate entry into the Great Room and dining area. There is also a partial kitchen, a half bath with Celtic decor, plus a back room for storage and extra supplies utilized for large gatherings. Throughout the Hearth, we sought to emphasize the global citizenship theme with art, creating a Latin American room, an African room, a corner Asian meditation center, a Northwest room, and a Library with a children's play area.

To the right of the rock stairs climbing to the Hearth from our home, there's an original root cellar with an enticing blue door. At the top of this three-tiered rockery we planted a Weeping Cherry, a gift from the English department where I was the director of Whitworth's Writing Program. Under the tree, a carver created a memorial from natural stone with her name, Krista Hunt Ausland, her birth and death dates, and the words "A Joy Forever."

First an angel and later a Saint Francis statue enhanced the space. Here blue forget-me-nots and bright yellow daffodils bloom in the spring, just in time for our annual Day of Prayer for Krista Colleagues held on May 20, the anniversary of her death. Later we discovered that the large deciduous tree hovering over the entire rockery is a Chinese tree, Ailanthus, that translates as "The Tree of Heaven." It seemed like a fitting sentinel for this garden's place of remembrance.

ABOVE Krista's favorite flower, the common daisy.

A Doorway into Thanks

"For all that has been, thanks;
for all that will be, Yes!"

~Dag Hammarskjöld

Chapter III

A Blessing for Comfort

"A sacred space, gracious, meditative,
soul-renewing and spirit recalibrating.
We've been given space to be held and nurtured
by the Holy Spirit. And given a world perspective
by all the magical art, tapestry
and stain glass. We've been deeply blessed."

~MIKE AND CAROL HASS
CELEBRATING THEIR 49TH WEDDING ANNIVERSARY

For Comfort:

When Your people need comfort, may the peace in this soul space and these gardens offer healing and hope, giving visual assurance that God hears the brokenhearted, offering the Biblical promise that You will turn our mourning into dancing and clothe us with joy, so that we will give thanks to You forever.

There's a visual mellowing of the land as fall comes to the Hearth gardens. The Sunset and Japanese maples, witch hazels, barberry bushes, marigolds, and sunflowers all shimmer with burnished shades of gold, amber, chocolate, green, and wine. Tall grasses wave in the growing winds while the crisp air hints at the cold winter ahead. But for a few glorious weeks, guests enjoy nature's grand farewell before the season of rest.

In the fall of 2001, we found ourselves with a growing excitement as the decisions and finishing touches in this space emerged. We never commissioned major architectural drawings since by code we needed to stay similar to the barn footprint. However, we asked our Spokane friend Don Neraas, an architect utilized by the Episcopal diocese for churches and retreat centers around the world, to help us creatively design within our constrained space. Then our builders, Dave and Scott Baker, and their talented interior designer Janet Jones, implemented and enhanced the ideas.

Our first challenge? How do we maximize comfortable seating for larger gatherings? By placing a long padded window seat across the three Great Room windows, our seating expanded by ten, without the need for bulky chairs. Then the hunt began for a long antique harvest table to add character to the room. However, most were either badly cracked or far too expensive. But one day we found a warm honey table constructed out of antique pine floorboards from an Irish distillery. To further conserve space, we built another long padded bench against the west wall to provide permanent seating for one side of the table.

Comfort proves pivotal to encouraging people to linger for conversation during and after meals. So our next search was for chairs for the other side of the table and two ends. Jim traipsed into many a furniture store to test out affordable and durable chairs suitable enough for men his size at 6'2". Now the harvest table easily seats 12 to 14 and we can add a few extras, if needed. For bigger gatherings, such as Krista Colleague weekend retreats, we set up a long folding table and chairs in front of the other window bench. It's always a pleasure to see this quest for comfort prove worthwhile when we see guests tarry in conversation, sometimes for hours, after a meal.

The genuine stone fireplace anchors the room, similar to one I watched a Norwegian stonemason build in my childhood home. A long stone ledge in front of the fireplace provides more seating.

To the right of the fireplace, the architect soared the ceiling to the top of the second level, and added upper windows. Glass doors beneath lead to the Latin American patio, allowing for a sense of spaciousness and light. In May, from the Great Room one can view a spring flowering tree that bursts into full blossoms of white. This seems especially charming when a red robin rests on branches of the tree.

To the left of the fireplace, a stained glass circle window with the Krista Foundation logo often reflects radiant light within the wall next to the fireplace. Artist Spike Grosvenor, a retired professor of stained glass, wanted to create this stunning window as a gift. We entered a visual paradise while visiting his home studio where he collects exquisite glass from around the world for his commissioned projects. It felt like a feast day when he invited us to make our choices among so many magnificent colors that also held so much history in each piece. When the sunlight shines through the antique European glass, shades of red, gold, and deep blue sparkle on whomever is seated in the wingback chair beneath the window. It also lights up the carpet with whimsical rainbow hues.

For months, figuring out this logo for the Krista Foundation proved very elusive. We needed it for stationery, brochures, and more. But we didn't want to hire a branding graphic artist without a clear idea of what we wanted to

convey. One balmy evening, when Aaron was back visiting us, we sat out on the patio for dinner and wine. Jim and I lamented our inability to figure this out. "What do you want to communicate?" Aaron asked. We mentioned the *Joy Dance* theme, where volunteering isn't seen as a sober, serious way of being. After Krista's death, Aaron had spoken about this spirit. "We did the storybook thing, sold all our possessions, moved to Bolivia, filled with hope and promise. It was a lot of fun!"

In minutes, he drew *K* and *F* as two dancing figures. We knew immediately that this was our framework! Then, our daughter Susan's husband Peter offered to contact one of Chicago's finer graphic designers to take it from there. We were

BELOW Using antique European glass, stain glass artist Walter "Spike" Grosvenor created the Krista Foundation logo as a gift to the Hearth.

ABOVE Debriefing Retreats provide Krista Colleagues an in-depth opportunity to explore the impact of their volunteer experiences and develop ways to transform these experiences into a lifelong ethic of service leadership.

amazed when the designer added a mountain line behind the *K* and *F* figures, not even knowing the story of how Krista died in the foothills of the Andes.

Guests view the stained glass logo from two deep moss green corduroy couches, a relaxing fabric brightened with global woven pillows. We upholstered the long window and table cushions in a warm, multi-colored, sturdy fabric, knowing these would receive maximum wear and tear. A Mexican pine armoire houses the media and music system and the global music collection. A rocking chair created in Pennsylvania's Bird-

in-the-Hand Amish community and an antique bench from England provide more places to relax.

Our very first gathering came at Thanksgiving with extended family coming from Boston and Western Washington. Susan brought us a beautiful tapestry from Peru that graces the Great Room wall, and son, Jefferson, always a handy carpenter, built a two-level shoe rack for guests to change into slippers. By now, the acute rawness of Krista's death that left her grandmother, brother and sister, and Jim and me so devastated had begun to mellow. We could be together with laughter, music, and the building of new memories.

ABOVE A Mexican artist created this tile Madonna. While traveling, we look for global artistic expressions of the Christian faith.

In honor of the Irish harvest table, Jim bought some Guinness Stout and we toasted and cheered to this extended vision for the Krista Foundation. I was just beginning to embrace internally the wise words of Dag Hammerskjöld, once the Secretary-General of the United Nations, in his memorable spiritual diary *Markings*.

> *For all that has been, thanks;*
> *for all that will be, yes.*

Seeing this soul space come to life gave Jim and me comfort and a growing sense of healing peace in our shattered hearts.

Since the foundation is a legacy to Krista's memory and her source of vision and strength, we chose to let our faith roots grow deep and wide, with a broad ecumenical Christian foundation. Our Krista Colleagues come from many branches of Christian expression, from within Catholic, Protestant, or Anabaptist backgrounds. They serve all people throughout America and the world who may embrace many other faith traditions, or none at all.

Through art, we are looking for global expressions of the Christian faith to grace the Hearth. From Mexico, we discovered a colorful tile artist who created the scene of Jesus and his disciples at the Last Supper. Clearly within the Catholic tradition, the Madonna offers a message of comfort to believers, and the same tile artist created a Madonna and Child figure for a wall hanging.

There's also a small statue and photograph of the Black Madonna and Child from Montserrat, Spain, at our entryway welcome desk. According to legend, she was discovered by shepherds in a grotto in the 9th century, and she was believed to be hidden in 718 to avoid falling into the hands of the Moorish invaders. Some believe the present version is a Romanesque sculpture in wood from the late 12th century, perhaps replacing the original that had been damaged in wars.

Whatever the origins, the discovery of the ancient statue became the impetus for the building of a large church and monastery. Thousands of pilgrims and tourists visit the site outside Barcelona every year. Often our Colleagues who are Jesuit Volunteers know the story of Ignatius of Loyola who visited the Benedictine monastery in 1522 after his recovery from battle wounds. While there, he laid down his military accoutrements before the statue and eventually founded the Jesuit order. The Black Madonna received a canonical coronation on September 11, 1881.

> "What a time of comfort and healing at the Hearth with meals, shared laughter, and good conversation for my husband Keven and our little boy Gabriel. He will get to see 'God's love in actions' through the presence of my mentors and community. What more could I possibly ask?"
>
> ~ *Kayla Walker, Krista Colleague*

A Bishop Tutu doll from South Africa sits on a child's rocker near a large stone triptych of the Trinity and Creation. At a local juried art show, we met Sam Bates, a fine stone artist who lives in Eastern Washington. After several years of conversation sharing our vision for the Krista Foundation, he carved the triptych from Montana stone. Starting from the left side, he sought to tell a narrative. In a description to the side of the triptych, he writes,

> *I wanted the content of the design to progress from the abstract and mostly unknowable aspects of God to His presence as the Creator and sustainer of all life and moving ultimately by the third panel to a chalice, modeled after the famous Celtic Ardagh chalice in Ireland. This shows God's incarnational presence in our lives, which is the root of all joy.*

He used gold leaf to highlight his images of wind, wheat, fiery angels, clouds, rain, a butterfly, a chalice, and an empty cross. To represent God's Spirit, he chose an Arctic Tern, rather than a dove, because of its astounding migration that circles the entire globe. A pathway with tiny human figures represents how we are pilgrims walking in faith, all sojourners in life.

RIGHT A small statue of the Black Madonna from Montserrat, a major pilgrimage site in Spain.

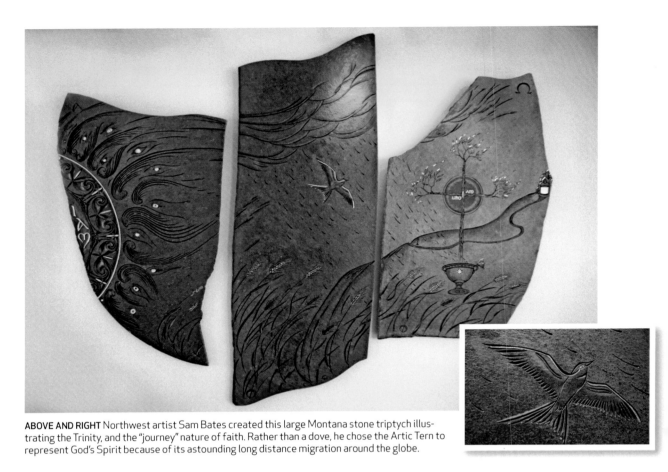

ABOVE AND RIGHT Northwest artist Sam Bates created this large Montana stone triptych illustrating the Trinity, and the "journey" nature of faith. Rather than a dove, he chose the Artic Tern to represent God's Spirit because of its astounding long distance migration around the globe.

The Great Room centers the hospitality of the Hearth. A framed photograph of an ancient Celtic Rune of Hospitality sits on a counter.

I saw a stranger yestreen
I put food in the eating place
Drink in the drinking place
Music in the Listening place
And in the Sacred Name of the Triune,
He blessed myself and my house,
My cattle and my dear ones,
And the Lark said in her song__
*   Often, often, often*
Goes the Christ in the Stranger's guise
*   Often, often often*
Goes the Christ in the Stranger's guise.

Over in the corner are several musical instruments such as African drums, a folk guitar, Latin American rattles, and wooden Andean flutes. Often guests, both skilled musicians and little children, pick up an instrument and start making music. It's also a space where several intimate house concerts have welcomed others. Eclectic global music adds vibrancy to gatherings, whether Maná from Mexico, Brazilian folk music, Miles Davis, U2, Medieval French chants, Bolivian pan flutes, Spanish flamenco guitar, or the unique voices of Angélique Kidjo or Miriam Makeba.

It is in the Great Room that the Krista Colleague cohort classes gather and meet for the first time each year. They come on the Friday

ABOVE Adults and children alike enjoy experimenting with the Hearth's collection of global musical instruments.

night before our annual Memorial Day weekend conference held at Clearwater Lodge, a Presbyterian camp and conference. The room is also where they come back together with other Colleagues after finishing their service assignments for Debriefing Retreats.

Our staff and board often use the Great Room for other planning or leadership training meetings, and Colleagues also come for personal visits when needing restoration, a thinking space for projects, or just a pause while traveling through Spokane. Many other guests and non-profits also find the Hearth to be a creative place for meetings, or a personal refuge of peace and natural beauty during life's journeys.

NATHAN PALPANT

In 2001, Nathan Palpant joined the first medical team to enter the war torn region of South Sudan in four years. Deeply disturbed by the suffering he saw, he used his Krista Foundation grant to return and videograph this forgotten land to raise awareness in America.

"I was wrestling with so many questions when I completed my year of service, but my sending agency only gave me a 30 minute debriefing session!" he said. So he and his wife, Darien, also a Krista Colleague, found Debriefing at the Hearth extremely valuable. "I needed this community to help process my confusion and pain." A talented writer, Nathan became the Managing Editor of our first *Global Citizen Journal*.

His time in Sudan left him debating his vocational aspirations and whether to drop his goal to enter medicine. Ultimately, he chose to become a research scientist, earning his Ph.D. from the University of Michigan. Now at the University of Queensland in Australia at the Institute for Molecular Bioscience, he provides leadership for a team researching potential breakthrough therapies for heart disease. However, his desire to understand human suffering and human dignity also persists and led to co-editorship of a book published by Oxford University Press, *Suffering and Bioethics*.

WATERFALL AND POND

When you look out the East windows of the Great Room, you overlook the Asian waterfall and pond. However, this garden was orignally much smaller, before we discovered the power of water as a balm for healing.

It happened that our daughter Susan's wedding to Peter Stevens was exactly one month from the day of Krista's death. She had planned for her sister to come up from Bolivia to be her maid of honor. Wedding invitations were already mailed for this big celebration in Newport, Rhode Island. "Should I cancel our wedding?" asked Susan when I had to call and give her the heart-shattering news of her little sister's death. "Let's hold on that decision until you and Peter are here," we suggested. "Our family might actually need this expression of joy."

Because we live on the West Coast and knew it would be difficult for local friends and family to attend, we had planned a garden wedding reception later in the summer. Her grandmother wanted to build a small pond and hillside waterfall in time for our Spokane celebration. Plans were already drawn and construction was beginning soon.

What we hadn't known then was how healing this oasis of water would prove in the year ahead. We often gathered near the water for long conversations with Aaron, other family and friends, or just to sit in the silence and solitude of grief. "He leads

LEFT The beauty of a Japanese water lily blooming in the pond.

me beside still waters, and restores my soul," the Psalmist declares in Psalm 23. This place became our still waters.

So after we built the Hearth, we decided to expand the size of the waterfall and pond to connect the hillside land with the gardens and our home below. Wanting to echo the global citizenship themes in the Hearth, we gave similar thoughts to the gardens and chose to center the Asian garden near the water.

We asked Ed Tsutakawa, who was instrumental in designing Spokane's authentic Japanese garden, to meet with Alderwood Landscaping, the firm building our expanded waterfall and pond. We needed help integrating Japanese principles into the design. As a child Mr. Tsutakawa had lived in the Japanese internment camps during World War II, and as a young man, he lost his first wife in childbirth. He met with Aaron, sharing his similar story of having once been a young husband living in profound sorrow. We felt immensely fortunate that he engaged his great heart and mind in this modest home project.

"What you hope happens in time," he encouraged, "is the principle of *Shibui*. It's an elegant simplicity that comes as a garden ages... like moss on a rock." Through the use of nature, with plants, trees, waters, and rocks, shibui creates a tranquil or "energized calm" of stillness and solitude. This offers a space for peaceful contemplation, often becoming a spiritual haven for visitors.

We followed his guidance about the concept of three, with a dominant rock and two smaller ones placed in relationship. In traditional Asian gardens, the tallest rock often represents heaven, the shortest rock is the earth, and the medium rock is humanity, the bridge between heaven and earth.

Through the principle of asymmetry, he advised avoiding straight lines. So he included two connected ponds, one oval and one semi-round, united with a stone bridge to walk across.

RIGHT A stone lantern in the Japanese Yukimi tradition, also known as a snow-viewing lantern, lights up the pond each evening.

LINDSAY LEEDER

"Volunteering with indigent AIDS patients in a Houston Hospice completely rocked my understanding of life," recalls Lindsay Leeder, a Jesuit Volunteer. "Watching persons in their last days on earth, often alone, broke my heart over and over. It felt like I was in a mystical thin space."

At Seattle University, Lindsay had been an outstanding pre-med Sullivan scholar, and a varsity soccer player.

She found service a humbling challenge to the ego. "No matter how hard I worked to care for someone, they still died. No longer did I live with the illusion I could control everything."

"When I came to the Hearth for debriefing, I was jaded and frustrated with community work. As we told stories and unpacked our experiences, I saw this differently." She became aware that this life is the only one she had, and began asking herself, What do I want to do with it? "I realized my heart didn't just break; it broke open, increasing my capacity to love beyond anything I first imagined."

This reconfirmed her commitment to compassionate health care as a Nurse Practitioner, first in family practice, and now as a Clinical Consultant with Vera Whole Health, founded by Krista Colleague Ryan Schmid.

Evergreen trees in different shapes and textures, including a Korean pine, accent the pond and symbolize strength and endurance. The stone lantern creates an artistic focal point and at night gives light to the tall iris, grasses, and lily pads that bloom in the summer.

The garden was completed just in time for our son Jefferson's wedding rehearsal dinner. We adopted Jefferson from Korea when he was almost five, and we were thrilled that he had found a deep love with Kris, a remarkable single mother raising three daughters. Celebrating this joyous moment in an Asian garden seemed honoring.

"Energized or active calm" certainly describes this space that draws our guests to relax in red wicker chairs around the pond and circle fireplace. Watching robins and finches

"What a refuge! This place has a very special spirit. Shelter from the storm and then the aromas of the gardens, darting and floating butterflies, music, wonderful food. The sunrise. So beautiful!"

~ Parker Logan

"The sacred energy of the Hearth and the beauty of the surroundings have been balm for the tender places still smarting over the loss of both my father and mother. I can't imagine anything worse than losing a child, but this helps me see how the light of love, compassion and God's grace can infuse even the darkest tragedy."

~ *Sondra, guest*

OPPOSITE (top left) Discovering the gold fish and frogs amidst the lily pads offers a favorite search for children visiting the gardens. **ABOVE** Our "campfire" on the patio offers another gathering place for guests near the pond.

splash and refresh in Spokane's summer heat, discovering goldfish swimming among the lily pads, or listening to the mating calls of vocal frogs in the spring (a noise that can actually drown out patio conversation) enlivens the spirit. Two burnished metal blue heron echo the rare visits of a real heron that sometimes threatens the elusive goldfish. On a piece of driftwood from Whidbey Island, Jim's father carved a girl blowing in the wind. She rests near a lacy magenta maple and reminds us of the heritage of family that enriches our lives.

In May, a Star Magnolia blooms with white petals, and a rose quince and copper red lace leaf maple soften the rocks. Above it all, an interesting tiered maple turns brilliant colors in the fall. Ferns, hostas, and sweet woodruff add gentle beauty, along with tall yellow columbine, that bloom for weeks.

Now, years after creating this space, when we see the moss gently covering the pond rocks and a single exquisite water iris bloom, we remember Mr. Tsutakawa and feel shibui. An "energetic calm" for all souls. ⌇

You CAN TRUST ME.

Love, God

inspired by
Numbers 23:19

Chapter IV

A Blessing for Counsel

"My heart has taken me places
my mind never imagined I'd go."

~Words from Tupou Ana,
a 2005 Krista Colleague who journeyed from the
Pacific Islands to Pasco, Washington, where he worked
as a para-educator with at-risk children.

LEFT This Biblical quote rests against a strong Ponderosa Pine
across from prayer chairs in the Secret Garden.

For Counsel:

During times when decisions confront us, may this soul space provide moments of quietude and contemplation, giving us a chance to hear ourselves and receive Your guidance, experiencing the Psalmist's wisdom:

> I bless the Lord who gives me counsel; in the night also my heart instructs me. I keep the Lord always before me... Therefore my heart is glad, and my soul rejoices, my body also rests secure.
> You show me the path of life.

As we find insight by listening to ourselves and You, may we also grow in learning to listen to others, with attentiveness and welcome.

What do I do now? What's next?

All of us enter times where we long for wise discernment when making decisions. But Krista Colleagues are in their twenties, and these are the years when significant life choices often especially shape their future trajectories. When they first complete their volunteer service, unless it was within their home community, they immediately face the challenges of finding a place to live, finding a temporary job during transition time, and finding or renewing friendships.

But major decisions loom too. Most ponder next steps around professional discernment. Whether they sense a need for further skills gained through work experiences or graduate studies, questions abound. Some also ponder local involvement in community activism, commitments with a life partner, or becoming a parent. Plus, like everyone else, they have the daily choices around family, friendships, health, neighborhood, and community.

Each decision calls for intentionality in listening.

However, we live in a noisy and wired culture that makes moments of quiet contemplation, a time to hear our deeper self, actually rare. Because of this, during their first year back home, they are invited to an extended weekend at the Hearth for our Debriefing Retreats. During this gathering, the staff and older Colleagues present ways of listening to oneself and enhancing listening skills towards others. We also introduce spiritual tools

ABOVE Meaghan Driscoll, a Krista Colleague, in contemplation during a Debriefing Retreat. She served in Spokane's St. Margaret's shelter for homeless women before attending Gonzaga University Law School on a Thomas More scholarship.

that develop practices for contemplating the sense of God in their lives. This resonates with Episcopal priest and contemplative author Cynthia Bourgeault's concept that "paying attention to one's heart" helps one live with "intention in life."

Some Colleagues return from their volunteer experiences burned out by the depth and scope of the world's needs, and they recognize the importance of a personal pause to restore their resilience and hope. But they also carry a ripening awareness that their skills and talents are genuinely needed in this wounded world. So most still harbor a compelling desire to create a meaningful life that includes contributing to others.

But how? And where?

Many Colleagues find that when they first complete their service assignment, the rush and daily demands of American life keep them from thinking or talking much about what happened during their service journey. It can almost feel like a "been there; done that" experience. A closed story. They often mention that peers and even family rarely want to hear much of their deeper experiences.

"When illness forced me to return home early from the Peace Corps in Africa, my college friends were just glad I came home safe after a medical evacuation," recalls Sinead Harris. "They just wanted to go out, have fun, party, and not dwell on difficulties. It was a disorienting time when I felt like such a failure."

Like other Colleagues, Sinead expresses immense gratitude for the Debriefing Retreats the Krista Foundation offers. This gave her the first chance to genuinely plumb her Peace Corps experiences, her unsettling questions, and her growing sense of loneliness. Sinead worked as an HIV/AIDS and family planning educator within the community health clinic in the Ethiopian town of Welenchiti, a name that means "broken promise."

The name captured the reality of this very remote town located on the high volume truck route for Middle East trade. "The town was overwhelmed with truck drivers, prostitutes, orphans, and AIDS," recalls Sinead. "I really valued the growing friendship with the commercial sex workers trying to generate an alternative income and lifestyle. When I was facing renal failure and severe dehydration because of a water shortage, I had to leave suddenly without even saying goodbye. It was devastating." After a month of recovery in a South African hospital, Sinead's health crisis ended her time with the Peace Corps.

"The only people I ever opened up to were my fellow Colleagues," recalls Sinead. "I wasn't getting blank faces at my pain, but rather comforting words. Feeling like someone could relate was the greatest gift. Finally the loneliness and depression lifted." When Colleagues begin telling their stories to one another, they find genuine companions on their way. They often discover a rich reservoir of life-altering perceptions once they are encouraged to access these as an important part of their service journey.

Listening to Others: Mutual Invitation Process

Although they begin with a cohort class, Debriefing Retreats often include Colleagues who have never met because they complete their service assignments at different times. Within any new group, there are a variety of communication styles. Some persons might feel more comfortable engaging in discussion while others are more hesitant to share. Out of respect for the growing diversity within the Krista Colleague community, they are introduced to the "Mutual Invitation Process" during focused group discussion times.* This innovative way of speaking and listening helps create a space where everyone has a chance to be involved and heard. Developed by the founder of the Kaleidoscope Institute, Eric H. F. Law, his intensive leadership program provides multi-cultural training for a diverse, changing world.

In his book *The Wolf Shall Dwell with the Lamb,* Law describes how the typical group opens a discussion where anyone can volunteer to speak. His research shows that this "volunteer style" of interaction within group settings favors some, but excludes others. This usually relates to differences in patterns of communication influenced by culture, gender, personality (such as introvert or extrovert), or age. So he developed this commu-nication tool where everyone is invited to speak without interruptions or refutations until everyone has spoken who wants to speak.

"It helps everyone," believes Stacy Kitahata, who initiated this process as our Program Director. "Our extroverts who typically process externally mention that the chance to 'pass for now' gives them time to think first. Knowing the group will circle back eliminates the need to fight to get into the conversation. For other Colleagues, especially those more reticent to jump in, there is an assurance that all voices will be valued and invited to contribute. It builds more equity." The Mutual Invitation tool also models a process Colleagues could find useful when they offer future leadership with other diverse groups in their communities or workplaces.

During the extended Debriefing weekend, the staff balances private times of reflection, times of relaxation, and times to gather, usually centered on a particular topic. A favorite evening includes Colleagues sharing a photograph and story about a meaningful relationship.

Each Colleague has been asked to bring a picture of "someone they still carry in their heart." During this fascinating evening, they share a portion of their service story and explain how knowing that person influenced them then and now.

BELOW Staff member Becky Collier (left) provides pivotal communications and systems administrative assistance, and Stacy Kitahata leads outreach with partner organizations across the country.

*See fuller description in the NOTES section in the back.

ABOVE Krista Colleague Glenn McCray shares a story at a Debriefing Retreat after serving with Urban Impact's tutoring and leadership programs in Seattle.

Spencer Uemura, who volunteered with the Jesuit Volunteer Corps at a Native American reservation in Montana, shared one such story of his friendship with a third-grade boy. "He was a large, strong kid, with a big personality. He was also a bully, a difficult child in the classroom. In a way he seemed threatening, not directly, but I imagined my third-grade self meeting him when I was quite small."

But as Spencer saw experienced teachers encourage the boy to see himself as a "protector" and to use his strength and power to help people, the child gradually changed. Then Spencer attended his first Pow Wow. "Seeing my young friend in his golden regalia, hearing him sing his tribe's sacred songs, and stamping his dance with so much pride and experience, I saw his cultural strength. He taught me a lot about the complexity of a child, and I grew to love him." Seeing these

photographs hung by the fireplace and hearing their stories offers a glimpse into a Colleague's pivotal moments in service. Sometimes beautiful, sometimes heartbreaking.

After Colleagues have shared stories, they explore together, "What resonated? What surprised you? What left you pondering?" They notice the commonalities and distinctiveness across their very diverse service journeys, whether in Burkina Faso, urban Chicago, or their home communities like Tacoma or Seattle, Washington. They also address what new insights into their service experience arise from listening to these companions. How has their worldview been challenged, or affirmed? By the end of these gatherings, Colleagues have traveled together across America and the world and forged friendships of understanding that often continue for years.

"The Debriefing retreat gave me the space to truly reflect on my year of service. I left my service experience extremely angry and these last few days have been re-energizing, rejuvenating, and most importantly, healing. I can't imagine how I would have worked through all of my emotions without the support of other Krista Colleagues who accept all of me—my hurt, pain, and love of service within this safe, welcoming, loving space."

~Krista Colleague

Listening to Yourself: The Journey Ahead

Besides listening to others, Colleagues are encouraged to take time to understand themselves more. Before leaving for service, new Krista Colleagues take the Intercultural Development Inventory, commonly known as the IDI and used by organizations in over 40 countries. This tool is utilized to provide cross-cultural competence through assessment, development, and guidance when persons communicate with those in another culture. After Colleagues take the IDI, our trained and certified staff offer to meet with them individually to provide feedback from this tool. This often proves insightful for their entrance into new cultural communities. "We seek to give them enough support to take risks," said Stacy Kitahata, "and enough challenges to grow."

For Lauren Davies, who volunteered in Costa Rica, the IDI gave her a lens to understand her experiences in Central American cultures that she still uses every day back in theUnited States. When she returned, her language skills in Spanish opened doors to a staff position with the Make a Wish Foundation. Each day she accompanies families in crisis over a child's dire health prognosis, and many are Spanish speaking families from small towns in the Eastern Washington region.

"Without the IDI, I doubt if I'd be as sensitive or respectful of differing cultural expressions of grief that we see daily. For example, when a Hispanic child is in the hospital, the entire extended family will often crowd into a hospital room to visit. The high value of community support proves central as they come to offer strength and hope. In my cultural background, unless we are close family or friends, we could be inclined to stay away and not interfere, or to take turns in hospital visits so as not to overwhelm."

When Colleagues return, another helpful resource includes learning of the seminal work on Adaptive Leadership theories from Dr. Ron Heifetz, co-founder of the Center for Public Leadership at Harvard University's John F. Kennedy School of Government. He emphasizes the value in recognizing what still remains important from one's earlier years during these young adult years of rapid change. As Heifetz states, "It's not just about change. It's also about identifying what you want to hold onto. Many leaders forget to remind people that a change process involves a lot of hard thinking about what to preserve."

For Nathan Williams, a Krista Colleague in the Class of 2008, listening to himself became extremely important after his pivotal years of living in an impoverished village in Burkina Faso while in the Peace Corps. An outstanding physics graduate, he entered one of the world's most prestigious Theoretical Physics graduate programs in Munich, Germany, after completing his service. But the memory of Burkina Faso citizens struggling with their lack of life's basics, such as electricity, stayed alive in his heart. After a

BELOW Krista Colleague Eli Burnham, seen here attending a Debriefing Retreat, served with QUEST, a Quaker organization, assisting in the food program with Lifelong AIDS Alliance.

semester in Germany, he returned to a Debriefing Retreat, and also met with his college science mentor, Dr. Kamesh Sakaran.

As he pondered his future, he recognized that, after seeing the profound hardships in the lives of so many, he really wanted to pursue Applied Physics. "I realized I wanted my technical expertise and education to make a useful contribution to solving problems now." He was particularly interested in the use of solar panels to provide electricity in villages like the one where he served in Burkina Faso. So he utilized his $1000 Krista Foundation Service Leadership grant to attend an international conference on solar energy in South Africa. Listening to his compelling vision, he left Germany to enroll in South Africa's fine Applied Physics program at Nelson Mandela University. While studying, he also met his future wife Mihloti, another excellent student.

His story is not an anomaly. Very often, one of the benefits of a year or more of valuable volunteerism is the clarification of what one's sustaining genuine interests and talents are. And are not. A shift in career focus, now motivated by intrinsic clarity of purpose, leads to a change of direction. Seeking discernment is part of the scaffolding of the entire Debriefing curriculum.

Yusuf Word knew his three years committed to mentorship offered an effective influence for at-risk teenage men of color in urban Tacoma who were very vulnerable to gang life. But he increasingly recognized that what gave him the greatest passion was his fascination with video and film production. He often created video projects with the students he mentored and for the Tacoma Urban League where he was a Youth Development Specialist. "They gave me a good camera with video capabilities to share their stories. I'd spend hours after work on their computers teaching myself essential technology and communication skills to improve my filming efforts. But I didn't see it as a career path immediately."

YUSUF WORD

Since moving to San Diego, Yusuf Word has worked as a video editor with Lyon and Associates Creative Services, honing his skills in design, illustration, and animation. "I loved drawing as a kid. It gave me peace and is a different kind of problem solving and way to use one's brain."

To begin his dream to get into film, he thought, "If I can just get on a set doing *anything*, I can begin." So he began his new career by freelancing in the film industry in Portland, Oregon, doing a lot of grunt work such as taking out the trash and even cleaning port-a-potties. But his start allowed Yusuf to slowly work his way up to several tv shows, commercials and movies, eventually learning how to edit.

Looking back on the past seven years, he likes that he's taken risks. "When I sensed that God was encouraging me to follow my heart's counsel, it seemed important to trust this. While learning new skills, rather than feel I'm not good enough for the challenge, I feel called to 'go for it.' I push through my insecurities since I've been given this blessing of a creative mind."

We benefited from this spirit when Yusuf created one of his first animation films for the Krista Foundation. "I don't want to live with regrets that I didn't have the courage to try. It's an exciting journey!" ❧

LINDA PAK

After serving with Presbyterian Young Adult Year in Mission with children of migrant workers and Native youth from the Yakima Indian Reservation, Linda Pak earned her graduate degree in Architecture at The Ohio State University.

"What I love about architecture is the chance to 'reimagine' new worlds, not just inhabiting a building, but asking questions on the way we live and how we would like to live together. This includes a cultural expression."

Working with Hoshide Wanzer Architects in Seattle, she especially valued designing public projects, such as parks and remodels at the University of Washington. "I love the process with public projects, even though it's longer and more complicated with many persons involved."

Every day she finds the professional service-leadership skills she's gained through the Krista Foundation immensely useful. "I've become far more aware of how I filter things. Also, rather than 'I'm the leader,' I've learned how to make decisions through consensus, and the importance of asking questions, such as 'Who is not at the table and how can their voice be heard?' This proves pivotal in public projects." She now resides in the beauty of Santa Fe, New Mexico, continuing with architectural design.

One afternoon while leading a discussion, he asked a group of high school students, "What do you dream of doing in your future?" Then, a sophomore turned it around and asked Yusuf what his career dream was. "I told her I wanted to be a movie director and she asked me, 'Well, why aren't you pursuing this?' Her words actually led me to consider this more seriously. Then, when I became a Krista Colleague, it was very encouraging to hear others in the Krista Foundation who supported my interest in film. They believed it also offered a place of profound contribution," said Yusuf. "That helped in making the leap to begin working with film companies."

For Megan Hurley Menard, a biology major, spending a year volunteering with a recuperative care program in Portland, Oregon, directly altered her future career. Her service involved helping homeless men and women with acute needs who were being released from hospitals. "I couldn't imagine coming out of surgery and soon going back on the streets." This reality for her clients gave her insight into major gaps in American medical care. When she began in Portland, there were five beds available for the post-surgical homeless in only one hospital.

Megan used her $1000 grant to attend a Housing First conference in Washington D.C., where she met many other Portlanders involved with this innovative approach for the homeless. As a result of her efforts, in collaboration with others she met, by the time her year ended Portland had 26 beds available in five hospitals. This program continues, and more recent Krista Colleagues have continued what she helped establish.

Seeing these medical needs ignited a determination in Megan to go back to college to attain her nursing degree with an emphasis on care for women and babies. Now a Registered Nurse, she works with low-income new mothers through a Spokane community health program.

A young mother herself, part of her medical responsibilities include valuable home visits. "I love empowering mothers and helping them gain confidence in their important care for a child."

These detours and changes in direction disrupt original plans for some Colleagues. But after listening to their desires, a compelling interior drive launches and sustains their efforts. For Nathan, listening to his desire to improve daily life for people without even basic needs provided by electricity meant letting go of a prestigious academic opportunity in Europe, moving internationally to South Africa, and trusting that a future in Applied Physics would open doors to help others. For Yusuf, listening to himself meant a major move from his familiar and close community in Tacoma, Washington, to the risky unknown world of California's film industry. For Megan, it meant expenses and time for more years of undergraduate schooling even though she had already graduated from college with highest honors. They each believe that taking the time to really listen to their heart and mind, though challenging, led them to make a pivotal and deeply satisfying life decision.

Listening to God: The Faith Journey

As an ecumenical faith community, our Krista Colleagues come from various streams of Christian expression in our culture. Although they often use different language to describe their reasons for service, their spiritual understandings reflect their shared love of God.

For example, if nurtured in the Jesuit tradition, they often connect faith with social justice issues; evangelicals often speak of wanting to share the love of Jesus; Quakers share the importance of "living in the light." What they hold in common, however, are similar ways in which their initial faith understandings, often learned from

ABOVE Volunteer experiences in tough places inevitably lead to young adults wrestling with hard questions. The Krista Foundation offers a community where these questions are welcomed, respected, and explored.

family or faith communities, become challenged in young adulthood. This offers a healthy time to explore important theological questions and assumptions.

We see wisdom in writer and social critic James Baldwin's quote, "The questions which one asks oneself begin, at last, to illuminate the world." For some, especially with their twenty-something peers, there exists a distrust or disinterest in organized religion, particularly for those burned by the culture wars within Christendom. Also, since many of the organizations they volunteer with are not faith-based, the theological questions they wrestle with are never part of their agency's concerns. So the Krista Foundation offers a safe and supportive community to express and face their questions.

Through our programs, conference worship experiences, and informal conversations with others from this variety of traditions, Colleagues experience a community where encouragement is given to grow into an empowering, holistic,

and inclusive Christian faith. Many find that the strength and courage they draw from their vibrant faith help them face the complexities and challenges of contemporary life.

During Debriefing Retreats, we also introduce them to the Ignatian spiritual practice as one of the practical tools for discernment. Initially developed by Ignatious Loyola, a 16th century Spanish priest and theologian who became the founder of the Jesuit order, it has been a sustaining faith practice for over 400 years in many cultures. Some of our Colleagues who attended Catholic universities are familiar with the practice, in contrast to those coming from Protestant backgrounds.

Ignatious created the EXAMEN* to help people become aware of God's presence, and to seek God's guidance for major discernment questions. He encouraged the practice of five key elements each day, often before bedtime, to find God in the midst of everyday life. "I found this practice introduced at Debriefing gave a way for me to unplug and slow down, to pay attention and listen to the ways I see God in my life," said Rediet Mulugeta, an effervescent Krista Colleague who volunteered in Houston and Chicago with Mission Year before joining our staff. Originally from Ethiopia, she grew up in an evangelical home and church after coming to America as a child. "This has been so valuable for me, I even introduced this morning and evening spiritual practice to groups that came to see our justice work in our challenging southside Chicago neighborhoods."

Although the gathering at the Hearth during retreats includes these structured sessions, a lot of relaxed fun times emerge with casual conversations in the patios and gardens. Seeing these budding friendships begin and hearing later how they enrich Krista Colleagues' lives for years to come gives us immense joy.

ABOVE Pins on a map in the Hearth library show some of the 55 American cities and 60 countries where Krista Colleagues have provided service.

* SEE NOTES showing the steps for this practice.

"What an incredible gift of this space for our Debriefing Retreat. We experienced such openness and gratitude in our conversations that we walked away amazed! The Krista Foundation provides a unique way to connect with like-minded souls and I will be forever grateful!"

~ Keri Majerus, Krista Colleague

ABOVE The children of photographer Robin Brazill, Raven, Ryan and Ryder Chavez, enjoy discovering the books and toys in the library.

The Library

Overnight guests are housed in the global rooms upstairs, including our tri-purpose Library used for reading, rest, and children's play. Insights from significant voices can be influential for counsel and expanding imagination, so our library offers an inviting collection of authors and subjects. Some are biographies or autobiographies from well-known "rivers" of influence, such as Nelson Mandela, Dietrich Bonhoeffer, Jane Addams, Martin Luther King, Jr., Malcolm X, Hildegaard of Bingen, Kirkegaard, Mother Theresa, and C.S. Lewis. Others are fiction from major historical and contemporary writers.

But most are the "tributary" writers, addressing topics concerning Latin America, Africa, the Middle East, environmental ethics, social issues, gardens, nature, art, and spirituality. Children's multicultural books, global travel books, and guidance books on topics like playing chess, gardening with native plants, or creating Asian gardens are part of the collection as well.

The library walls give some historical background on the Krista Foundation for guests to see. A few newspaper articles that feature Krista Colleagues are framed on the wall, and a global map shows where Colleagues serve around the world. Photographs of some of our Krista Colleagues cohort classes line the wall behind a queen size hideabed.

"I love it here, it's MAGICAL."

~ Quinlen Stevens, 10 years old

ABOVE Plants flourish with Jim's nutritious compost. Whenever a plant needs special attention, his compost offers almost a magical restoration.

Windows look out on the orchards with their changing beauty through the seasons.

Many of our earlier Krista Colleagues are now parents, and we wanted their children to sense that the Hearth is for them too. A puppet collection from around the world and a theater stand encourage creative play for children where they showcase their imaginary stories.

WELCOME TO THE SECRET GARDEN!

When children play outdoors, discovering the Secret Garden adds to their delight. Hidden by a thriving cedar tree, bamboo plants, and English laurel, a *Welcome to the Secret Garden* sign bids guests to enter the winding stone path that leads to this inner garden room.

It becomes a magical place visited by the many children. On a rock ledge, a troll house

beckons our young guests to open a tiny door where they find surprise gifts. They then notice a few small fairies hanging among the shade-loving ferns, hostas, and cedar branches. In spring and summer, white nodding Anemone flowers line a pathway of old pavers embedded within Irish moss. Whenever children return to the Hearth, this Garden is the first place they run to visit! Some even leave sweet thank you notes for the generous troll. In the mysterious realm of childhood imagination, we hope the Hearth and gardens encourages their sense of wonder.

Even adults find the Secret Garden an enticing place, especially on the annual Krista Foundation Day of Prayer. In Spokane, we open the Hearth on May 20th for tea and scones and have baskets filled with prayer requests from Krista Colleagues serving in America and around the world. Another basket

OPPOSITE (bottom left) We enjoy sharing the Northwest and Hearth when grandchildren Hunter and Quinlen Stevens visit from Boston.

ABOVE/LEFT Five-foot high red lilies and a rare Bullocks Oriole nest in the Witch Hazel.

includes prayer needs for our annual upcoming Memorial Day Conference that is co-designed by Krista Colleagues and staff. Guests often explore the gardens and then find a comfortable place for private prayer. As guests turn the corner into the Secret Garden's inner room, a tin-sculpture dancing girl, our *Joy Dance* symbol, greets them.

While sitting in the red wooden Adirondack chairs, one can read a carving with the Biblical assurance, "You Can Trust Me, Love, God"; then below, in smaller font, it gives the Biblical reference, "inspired by Numbers 23:19." It seemed appropriate for the times of transition and uncertainty that come to us all. But these words seem especially relevant for Colleagues

ABOVE Visiting children, like our granddaughter Erin Hunt, love discovering gifts left in the troll house.

living in liminal space when they first complete their service. We hope it offers a measure of peace as they ponder an unknown future.

In late winter, the first harbinger of spring comes from the early blooming of a stunning Witch Hazel, often still dusted by snow. In spring, the fragrant clusters of yellow bells dangling from a Golden Chain tree, circled by daffodils, give their light scent. One summer, a nearby tree became home for a Baltimore Oriole who constructed her elongated hanging bird nest, a rare gift on the land. Five foot high stately red lilies bloom for weeks. In fall, the Witch Hazel leaves turn into a riot of sunset colors brightening the landscape. In winter, the land rests, a reminder of the renewal we all need. ❧

Chapter V

A Blessing for Challenges

"Whatever you believe you can do, begin it.
Boldness has genius, power, and magic in it."

~JOHANN WOLFGANG VON GOETHE

For Challenges:

When groups gather around the hearth for a common purpose, illuminate their vision to see the world with Your eyes for our homes, cities, and global communities. During times when the needs of this world can overwhelm, help us to remember the UN's Secretary-General Dag Hammarskjöld's words, "In our era, the road to holiness necessarily passes through the world of action." Sharpen our awareness of those particular areas where the boldness and energy of our active commitments, creativity, and passions can create a better world for others.

As a guest enters the Hearth, they may notice a small photograph on the entry wall. It shows our muscular son Jefferson rock climbing on a sheer cliff. Under the picture is the famous quote on boldness attributed to Johann Wolfgang von Goethe, the great German playwright and thinker.

Some cite a fuller passage. "Until one is committed, there is hesitancy, the chance to draw back. Concerning all acts of initiative and creation . . . the moment one commits oneself, then Providence moves too."

When young adults choose to commit and invest a year or more in tangible service, recognizing the importance of the "world of action," they encounter significant challenges. Many know that receiving an education is clearly a privilege, as is the luxury of taking a year or more to volunteer. Some of our Colleagues choose to serve in their urban home communities and reinvest their gifts of education locally. Others travel throughout America or the developing world with their volunteer agency's assignments. Either choice demonstrates they live with a reservoir of hope, trusting deep inside that their actions can make some difference.

However, we find that this spirit of hope also carries shadows of a downside. Too often, when one engages as a volunteer in a developing nation or an impoverished American urban environment, one can enter with a strong, even dominant, sense of "what I can give."

Before Krista Colleagues begin, one of the core service ethics principles we introduce to them is the idea of "mutual indebtedness." This simply is an encouragement to be very aware and open to all that they will receive from others in the communities they serve.

Tom and Valerie Norwood, charter members of the 1999 Krista Foundation Colleague class, learned the power of this truth on their first day arriving in Saba Saba, a small hillside town north of Nairobi, Kenya. Their responsibilities with the Presbyterian Year in Mission included working with entrepreneurial Kenyans at the Iridiro Dressmaking and Tailoring business.

As a young couple who would be staying for a year, they had been assured they could share a room together in one of the nearby houses. "The day we arrived we were greeted by Njeri, the principal of the school there," recalls Val. "She took us over to a little stone house with a brightly painted door, and three freshly painted rooms. 'This is where you'll be living,' she said to us. It was Njeri's home and she'd chosen to give this to us. Later we saw she had moved for the next year into a small one room house with a tin roof. Her

generosity astounded us and immediately reversed the idea of who was serving whom." The concept of "mutual indebtedness" infused their year.

Although we provide preparation prior to their service, we find the greatest challenges for many Colleagues occur after they complete their assignment. Many come to know people within communities who live with daily suffering and injustice. Whether volunteering alongside malnourished children, women trapped by the sex trade, undocumented women fleeing violence, first generation American high school students, or impassioned locals seeking to keep endangered turtles in a safe habitat, Colleagues now have friendships that make abstract issues come alive.

How does one sustain this spirit of hope that propelled the initial desire to volunteer? For it takes an abiding intrinsic hope, boldness, and humility to keep any of us involved. Our goal for Krista Colleagues includes fostering a lifelong ethic of service, civic engagement, and global consciousness. Too often, especially for young people in America, volunteerism becomes a resume-building interlude before "real life."

As an intergenerational mentoring community, we invite wisdom voices to many of our events, including the annual Memorial Day conference. Over the years, our keynote speakers, such as Knut Vollebaek, the Norwegian Ambassador from Norway, Father Greg Boyle, founder of the innovative gang intervention HomeBoy Industries, and Katharine Hayhoe, a leading climate scientist, have enriched our intergenerational conversations. They demonstrate the possibilities of influence and the challenges of sustaining lifelong commitments.

One wisdom voice for Colleagues when they become discouraged by the immensity of the world's challenges has come from writer David James Duncan, best known for two award-winning novels, *The Brothers K* and *The River Why*, and his non-fiction memoir *My Story as Told by Water*. His shorter essays are often featured in national anthologies, such as *Best American Spiritual Writing*, and we published two in our *Global Citizen Journal*. As a citizen activist especially concerned for the plight of wild salmon, the impact of our wars overseas, and environmental destruction of our "holy earth," he found himself discouraged by the immensity of national and international conflicts and slow resolutions. Rereading Mother Theresa, he found encouragement in her words, "We can not all do great things. But we can do small things with great love."

Her advice gave him permission to take time to play with his kids and go fishing again. A renowned fly fisherman, he actually lives Mother Theresa's advice while fishing. He speaks of the importance of "parsing the river," slicing off a tiny ribbon known as a feeding lane. This is often just a six inch strip on a huge western river like the Blackfoot that is three or four hundred feet across. It is here where he finds all the rising trout get hooked. For those who yearn to make a difference, he suggests applying this fly-fishing strategy. "Every morning, look for 'ribbons.' One small thing you sense could be done with full-on attentiveness and love. After you finish it, look for another." He calls this "direct small-scale compassion activism."

Rather than being overwhelmed by the immensity of problems, we encourage our Colleagues to learn how to balance active commitments with realistic awareness of our limits. The writings of Archbishop Óscar Romero, assassinated because of his bold support of the poor in El Salvador, illuminate this perspective. Remembering that a broad community of other persons is committed to the common good becomes a vital part of a lifelong healthy service journey. With realistic humility, this long view is expressed in the prayer attributed to Archbishop Romero.

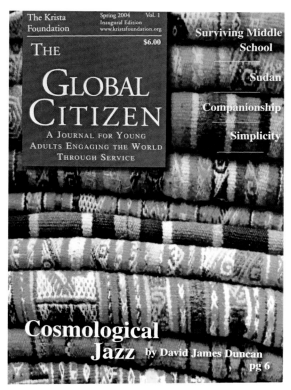

ABOVE Our first *Global Citizen Journal*, unique as a journal for young adults engaging the world through service.

Although we built the Hearth for the needs and purposes of the Krista Foundation, we knew from the beginning it could be expanded for others. As a creative center, the Hearth offers Spokane organizations a unique nearby gathering place. Like all cities, Spokane has engaged citizens who work diligently to create a better world. For these citizen leaders who contribute to vital civic organizations, churches, universities, and schools, the Hearth provides a place of beauty and peace where distractions are lessened. Our hope is the refreshing spirit of the Hearth and gardens contributes to creative thinking as they envision implementing their organization's mission, their particular "ribbon in the river."

Prophets of a Future Not our Own

It helps, now and then, to step back and take the long view.

The kingdom is not only beyond our efforts, it is even beyond our vision.

We accomplish in our lifetime only a fraction of the

magnificent enterprise that is God's work.

Nothing that we do is complete, which is another way of saying

That the kingdom always lies beyond us.

No statement says all that could be said.

No prayer fully expresses our faith.

No confession brings perfection, no pastoral visit brings wholeness.

No program accomplishes the church's mission.

No set of goals and objectives includes everything.

This is what we are about. We plant the seeds that one day will grow.

We water the seeds already planted, knowing that they hold future promise.

We lay foundations that will need further development.

We provide yeast that produces the effects far beyond our capabilities.

We cannot do everything, and there is a sense of liberation realizing that.

This enables us to do something, and to do it well.

It may be incomplete, but it is a beginning, a step along the way, an opportunity

for the Lord's grace to enter and do the rest.

We may never see the end results, but that is the difference between

the master builder and the worker.

We are the workers, not master builders, ministers, not messiahs.

We are prophets of a future not our own.

BELOW (left to right) This contemporary Biblical translation from Psalm 51, sent by Suzette and Terry McGonigal, offered comfort during the deepest months of grief. Danny Parker and Amanda Muchmore chose to do an August pre-wedding ceremony in the Hearth Gardens. They wanted Danny's mother, Pamela Corpron Parker, to share in their celebration. She died of cancer the next day.

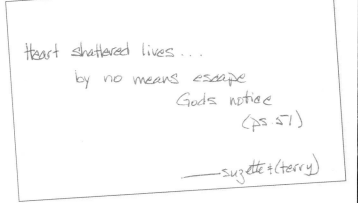

Heart shattered lives . . .
by no means escape
Gods notice
(ps.51)

——suzette & (terry)

A number of community organizations, such as Spokane's Interfaith Council, the Center for Justice, various church groups, St. George's School, the NAACP, Whitworth University's President's cabinet, and Gonzaga University's Center for Global Engagement, have found the Hearth to be a restorative meeting space.

The Hearth also welcomes many for family events. Some are times of joy; others times of sorrow. Whether celebrating joyful moments, such as anniversaries, birthdays, reunions, bridal showers, even weddings, or times of heart-shattering sorrow such as memorials, we've learned to live in these intertwined truths that all people carry.

Kahlil Gibran speaks of this fusion of love and sorrow in his classic book *The Prophet*. He writes, "Your joy is your sorrow unmasked. And the selfsame well from which your laughter rises was oftentimes filled with your tears. And how else can it be? The deeper that sorrow carves into your being, the more joy you can contain."

One memorable gathering in the gardens linked two deeply emotional moments of joy and sorrow in the summer of 2016. Only in her 50s, Pamela Corpron Parker was a very close friend and colleague in the English department at Whitworth University. For two courageous years, she endured the life-threatening challenge of melanoma.

Pam held a deep love for family, and her dream was to be at her oldest son Danny's wedding to Amanda Muchmore. She so longed to stay alive for their ceremony planned for mid-October. The challenge Danny and Amanda faced that summer was a growing realization that his mom would probably not live that long.

They responded to this with a creative pre-wedding ritual in the Hearth gardens, a place Pamela loved since she herself was a passionate gardener. Her own Asian-inspired garden became a treasured space to relax with family and friends who received the gifts of her generous hospitality.

OPPOSITE Though widely attributed to Archbishop Óscar Romero after his assassination, the original prayer was written by the Bishop Ken Untener.

With just a few family members present, including Amanda's parents who flew in from Colorado, a Lutheran pastor friend designed a short, meaningful ceremony. Guests dressed in wedding attire, and the bride's father even helped make his daughter a beautiful blush rose bouquet. Amanda proudly carried this as she confidently exchanged pre-wedding vows with Danny.

Their joyful spirits filled the garden during a festive dinner with parental toasts to celebrate the upcoming marriage. Dressed in a lovely blue silk sheath and a scarf that only partially hid the tumors around her neck, Pam glowed with an inner happiness. When she tired, her husband Rob took her home early. To her family's great surprise, she fell asleep, never fully woke, and died the next afternoon. Though this left us all in sorrow, we also felt deep gratitude. During her last moments on earth, Pamela basked in the ongoing love of family while enjoying a celebratory feast within the splendor of a garden, always her favorite place to be.

The African Room

Many of our Colleagues have found profound challenges and beauty while serving in African nations, so we created one of our global bedrooms as the African room. Jack Brace was another Colleague serving in Kenya with the Presbyterian Year in Mission at the same time as the Norwoods. While visiting the ancient seaside city of Lamu, a town with 23 mosques, the three of them met a group of excellent Muslim woodcarvers. They decided

BELOW (left) Brian Muchmore, the father of the bride, flew in from Colorado and helped design Amanda's bridal bouquet.
(right) Krista Colleagues commissioned Muslim woodcarvers in Kenya to create a Safari chair using symbols from Krista's life.

to commission a safari chair for the Hearth. Using symbols from Krista's wedding and memorial, the comfortable wood carved chair offers seating next to the trundle bed.

Later, Jack and Tom decided on a week-long return to Lamu, a fascinating UNESCO heritage site founded in the 14th century as one of the original Swahili settlements. They wanted to take woodcarving lessons from the carvers as a way to build friendships. They also wanted to learn more of the faith and culture of the Muslim community.

Above the Safari chair are paintings from Nicholas Sironka, a visual artist and Maasai cultural educator from Kenya who comes to Spokane occasionally to teach art classes. Former board member, Dee Giannamore's hand made quilt and a decorative 'mosquito net' invite children into a cozy corner for story telling. Children's books with African themes and wooden animals enliven a side table. A sliding door looks out to the orchard and the children's playhouse made with the original old barn wood by Kyle Bungee, a friend of Krista's.

THE AMERICAN ORCHARD

Our greatest gardening challenge has been the two-tiered orchard, the home of several apple, cherry, pear, and plum trees, plus a raspberry and blueberry patch. High on the terraced hillside sits a 50-year-old cherry tree whose rugged bark and shape add character among small newer trees. Occasionally, the beloved tree even produces an abundant crop of bing cherries. But its unreachable height means it primarily keeps the birds fed and happy.

Over the years in our zone 5 region, we've planted semi-dwarf Santa Rosa plums, Bartlett and Asian pears, Rainier cherries, and various apples. Always living with glimmers of hope, we still experiment by planting the hardiest peaches and apricots recommended. For two summers we tasted the rare sweetness of a sun-ripened peach. Too often they die, get diseased, or stop producing after one of our late freezes. However, we're trying again with another species of peach and a nectarine. We'll see if they survive.

Our raspberry and blueberry patches produce well, as do grapes certain years, especially vines planted along a fence over 50 years ago by previous owners. Jim makes a delicious grape juice that we freeze and bring out for breakfast on a snowy day, a tasteful reminder that the warmth of sun will come again. It's also a wonderful earthy addition to hot mulled wine on winter's evenings.

But problems with production persist. The coddling moth and maggot flies prove especially daunting with apple trees since we try to avoid using pesticides. One summer I put every single apple in a nylon footie, a suggested organic way to prevent infestations. No such luck. Every apple still was diseased and we left them for the deer. However, the Asian pear, peaches, blueberries, raspberries and aronia berries produced magnificently and were blemish-free!

For a few years, most trees on our highest tier garden failed to produce fruit at all. Knowing enough water had trouble reaching this hillside, we made efforts to improve the water system, weeded a wide circle around each tree more carefully, added fruit tree fertilizer and Jim's magic compost. We were rewarded the following spring with abundant blossoms. Yet, even now, when spring blooms look promising, an untimely freeze makes fruit arrival intermittent.

Since nothing tastes like a sun-ripened peach, or a crisp Asian pear, we now have planted edible plants and trees throughout the front yards too. I'm even trying a recommended hardy fig tree that actually produced our second year. Unfortunately, the tiny figs didn't ripen before the cold began.

"The flowers, the music, the waterfall, the Celtic prayer provided our faculty a setting conducive to great discussion and wonderful ideas as we focused on applied brain research and Service Learning classroom projects."

~Nancy Spencer, director of St. George's Lower School

But the fig tree has lived! Irrational hope always abounds. We keep trying, guided by the local Master Gardeners and government extension programs who provide free advice.

The "black gold" on our land comes from Jim's compost, a three-bin system that he attends to faithfully. Whenever I see a plant in trouble, or we want to transplant a challenging tree, I ask "please bring me your gold." Our understanding of both the physical and metaphoric richness of compost has come from Krista Colleague Sarah Wanless Zwickle, who took a Master Composting/Soil Builder class from Seattle Tilth. She wrote an insightful essay for our *Global Citizen Journal* called "Service Compost" that we have new Krista Colleagues read in preparation for the difficulties related to their service journeys.

A Division I basketball star, Sarah spent her college years at the University of San Francisco living and breathing competitive sports. The teams' reward was an exhilarating trip to the

ABOVE Jim built a three-box compost bin where he creates the rich "black gold" nourishing our garden beds.

WAKEFIELD GREGG

A member of the Charter Class of Krista Colleagues, Wakefield Gregg has always enjoyed creating warm hospitality. While in Tacoma, volunteering with urban youth including some gang members, he remodeled an old Craftsman home to live in the Hilltop community. His first major purchase? A long harvest table to comfortably welcome his guests!

A close friend of Krista and Aaron's from University of Puget Sound days, Wake wanted her story shared through music—both the tragedy but also her joy. Using his tax refund, he commissioned a song written and played by Children of the Revolution, a Seattle-based band of world musicians and singers. "We even said part of it needed to be danceable, a symbol of her joy dance." They debuted "Angeles de Bolivia" at Seattle's prestigious Benaroya Hall in concert, and we gathered at the Hearth to first hear it on their album. After the pathos, the song turns into highly joyful dance music that we've played at many Krista Foundation gatherings.

While in an MBA graduate program at George Fox University, he traveled to China and saw the significance of 26 million Chinese commuting on electric bikes. Inspired by this affordable, environmentally friendly transportation, he opened Portland, Oregon's original E-bike store. This growing business is highly regarded for excellent customer service, another extension of Wake's hospitality. ꝏ

CHRISTINA LI

Christina Li works in Washington D.C. for the U.S. Department of State's Office of Religion and Global Affairs. This office provides an open door to religiously affiliated communities and leaders who wish to engage with the U.S. State Department. It also provides guidance to our top leaders in government on the nexus between religion and foreign policy. Understanding the role religion plays in global conflicts, peacemaking, or the persecution of religious minorities proves pivotal.

A Krista Colleague in 2004 with a degree in economics from Stanford, her interest in international affairs strengthened during her volunteer time working for a microfinance organization in the Philippines. To further gain skills to contribute, she's also earned two master's degrees in international development and human rights law.

"I found my times at the Hearth absolutely eye-opening," she recalls, "because I wasn't familiar with other forms of Christianity. I'd never known any Mennonites or Jesuits. Meeting Colleagues where we share the heart of faith, but through different lenses, gave me the background that is now part of my daily work. This requires an understanding of the different ways religion is believed and practiced within Protestant, Catholic, Muslim, Jewish, and other communities." ❦

NCAA's Sweet 16 her sophomore year. Her life was profoundly influenced by a chance visit to a vibrant and welcoming Methodist congregation in San Francisco, where 95 percent of the worshippers came from the South Pacific Island of Tonga. "Their music, language and passion combined to help me understand that Christ lived a passionate life of justice. In one swift heartbeat, I knew I wanted to live that kind of life."

After graduation for the next three years, this pivotal faith experience led her to choose a variety of intense volunteer opportunities. First, through the United Methodist church, she served as a young adult youth minister with disinterested teenagers in rural England. Then, she returned to Seattle and volunteered at a drop-in center for street kids in downtown Seattle. "I went full steam in volunteering, like I was in pre-season training, only this time I told myself I was 'getting in shape for God.' My goal was to be a superstar servant, a 110 percent volunteer. Impressing others through competition was the only solid framework I had to build on."

Eventually she discovered her competitive spirit only distracted her from the emptiness and uncertainty she felt, threw her life into imbalance, and led to an eating disorder. Because of her health, she took a pause and stopped volunteering for a year. Sarah grew up on a farm in Goldendale, Washington, and fond memories of her love of rural life reemerged.

Then she discovered the S&S Service Compost Homestead Farm and Educational Center on Lopez Island, a tiny island in Washington's San Juans where she interned for six months. Turning the compost regularly, she marveled anew at how garbage, properly attended, emerged as rich soil. She began relating this to her own life.

"When my season of service came to an end, I had a lot of leftovers. I recognized I had to create time and space and 'be still.' I needed a transformation. Like garbage in a compost pile, my service leftovers sat stacked on every available counter space, waiting to be changed from a polluting presence into a rich, life-altering and nourishing resource. I come from five generations of farmers. Tending the soil is woven into my design. The rhythms of digging, releasing, placing, firming, watering, and tending give my hands and mind a peaceful occupation."

When Sarah attended a Debriefing Retreat at the Hearth, she recalls, "This gave me an opportunity to turn my pile of service compost that I thought had grown cold. Through conversations and reflections, ideas and beliefs I had forgotten resurfaced, and I sent convictions and stale dreams back into the heart of my experiences to re-ignite them. I had given myself time to cool from the initial burn of service. Now I could uncover the leftovers that paralyzed me. The youth program I left unfinished in England, hopelessness walking the streets of Seattle, my eating disorder, questions about my images of God."

These reflections sparked insights into her journey. "The patience needed for compost, I started to give myself. I came to realize that my passions were planted by God. God wove into my heart all the things that made it skip, swell, ache, and beat. Following my innermost desires is not a betrayal of faith, but rather a germinating expression of the person God designed me to be." Sharing her essay, also published in our *Global Citizen Journal*, gives permission for other Colleagues to see and name the complexity of their own service journey. It also provides a lens for healthy acceptance of the hard parts of the inevitable challenges ahead. ✑

RIGHT For our tenth anniversary, Krista Colleagues created symbolic squares for bedding, and Dee Giannamore, a former Board member and talented seamstress, quilted the squares for the African room.

THE SIMPLE PATH
The fruit of silence is prayer
The fruit of prayer is faith
The fruit of faith is love
The fruit of love is service
The fruit of service is peace
—Mother Teresa

Chapter VI

A Blessing for Conversations

"Service is the entryway—
the hallway leading to the grand ballroom
of kinship, of being one with the other.
Jesus was not 'a man for others';
he was one with them.
There is a world of difference in that."

~Father Greg Boyle,
Founder of HomeBoy Industries
for gang intervention in Los Angeles

For Conversations:

When friends share this communal space, may it help forge the foundation of friendships, drawing us into the companionship our Creator desires. Lift forth our best selves around the feasting of table, fun, art, music, and natural wonder. May Your spirit abound in conversations around the pond and waterfall, on patios, in the Great Room, the library, and wanderings in the garden. Thank you for the gifts of intellect and heart that you generously give. May this Hearth become one place of belonging for people from around the world and for people serving around the world.

When Krista and Aaron awoke each morning in their small adobe home in Bañado de la Cruz, they grew to understand how the blessing of conversations proved pivotal in building friendships with the citizens in their community. What they learned ultimately shaped one of the blessings we desire for Krista Colleagues and guests visiting the Hearth.

Their mission in this isolated river village was something MCC called "accompaniment." Based on their years of development work, MCC didn't let volunteers initiate plans and launch projects. Instead, they were to accompany the community in their own choices for development. "I wasn't really sure how to do this," recalls Aaron, "how

to translate the mission into items on my typical to-do list."

On days when no clear task was before him, Aaron would just go out the front door and begin walking down the one dusty road that passed through town. "Often, someone would invite me over to sit for a while with them, even share a cup of hot tea. Sometimes we'd talk about one of the projects we were working on—honey bees, dry latrines, or accounting at the farmers' co-op. But more often we'd just talk about life, our families, and they'd ask how Krista and I were adjusting to life in Bañado."

It was from these casual conversations, where he admitted his and Krista's vulnerabilities, that kinship began. He became honest about their struggles living in a home without electricity or running water, not knowing the language or customs well, getting sick and suffering minor injuries, and actually feeling pretty useless.

"After some time, I realized that something else was happening over tea," recalls Aaron. "My title and position as a community development volunteer was eroding as I was becoming real to them. And my simplistic stereotypes of the poor were melting away. I saw them as strong, resourceful people whose resilience in a tough place demanded my deepest respect."

He also saw how much he and Krista depended on their generosity and friendship as neighbors gave them food from their lands and taught them about local plants to heal their bodies. "Over tea, we built trust and became vulnerable together. I was given insider knowledge of the community and the complex social rules and history that governed it. It made all the difference in the quality and impact of our time together."

Krista gained a similar understanding of the importance of conversations. While cooking on her porch with the women's cooperative, visiting women in their homes to learn how to bake bread in stone ovens, or discovering what herbal remedies help with common illnesses, she became a genuine part of their community.

In an email describing what Bolivians were teaching her, she wrote:

> I am learning a lot about our task-driven culture versus a relationship-based culture. Family is definitely the priority here (it's often expressed in sexist ways, but it's still definitely a priority). From the developmental standpoint, when we come into a community and focus on the work, the task, the achievements, and don't invest in the relationships, our being there is almost worthless in the eyes of those we meet.

THE GLOBAL CITIZEN
SPECIAL EDITION
A JOURNAL FOR YOUNG ADULTS ENGAGING THE WORLD THROUGH SERVICE

STAYING FOR TEA
Aaron Ausland
Five Principles for the
Community Service Volunteer
P.14

SERVICE COMPOST
Sarah Wanless Zwickle
Finding Healing in the Process
P.42

HOUSEHOLD ECONOMICS
Sharon Parks Daloz
Practicing Purposeful Living
P.58

THE VOICE OF THOSE WHO SING
Father Gregory J. Boyle
Impacting One Life at a Time
P.70

ABOVE The Krista Foundation created our fifth *Global Citizen Journal* to include the "most valued" essays from earlier volumes for organizations utilizing young adult volunteers and universities with international programs.

Her open spirit in building relationships became a core mission. "My wife cried for three days when she heard Krista died," one of the farmers told Aaron, "she was such a friend."

From the citizens of Bañado, Aaron and Krista learned the immense value of conversations, both casual and deeply intentional. This now shapes our gatherings at the Hearth where we hope guests find this a place of belonging. It also informed the concept of "Staying for Tea," one of the bedrock Krista Foundation principles preparing Colleagues for service.

From the beginning, we desired to create a space that celebrates a sense of community and trust. This begins on Friday night when the new cohort class arrives at the Hearth for their Memorial Day Retreat weekend. Though they share a

ABOVE The Latin American courtyard has three patios and tables for gatherings or small group discussions.

common desire to commit to service, Colleagues often come from very different life experiences in their economic, racial, social, and academic backgrounds. Some appear to be fairly relaxed when they arrive, anticipating the conversations ahead. Others are more reserved, waiting to see what this community is going to be like.

World music adds energy, and a few older Colleague mentors and staff greet the new Colleagues. Those who arrive early are invited into the kitchen to help chop, peel, and create their first dinner together. Soon the din from new conversations buzzes in the Great Room and spills out into the Latin American patio.

When all the evening programs have ended, I love seeing clusters of Colleagues enjoying each other as friendships begin. Some pick up the

musical instruments—guitar, hand drums, or their own instruments—and begin playing together. Others may start a chess game, or just relax in conversations with others in the gardens and patios.

As we welcome new Colleagues into the Krista Foundation community, our hope is this will launch the first of many important conversations at the Hearth, at our conferences, and informally as Colleagues forge friendships with other potential citizen leaders. For many, the initial introductions spawn the start of strong friendships with others who encourage their best selves.

This happened for Taylor Tibbs, who describes herself as an introvert, and now speaks of the Hearth as a second home. She remembers walking into the Hearth to meet her cohort class the first time. "I was worried," she recalls. "I knew I

ALICIA FAVREAU

One of our earliest Krista Colleagues, Alicia Favreau, has been instrumental within the Hearth and gardens from the beginning.

Alicia helped organize work parties in the gardens, helping make decisions on trees and plantings. But it was the kitchen where new Colleagues often saw her making a fresh garden rhubarb cobbler, or an overnight egg soufflé dish for a big breakfast. "My favorite time during retreats was cooking in the kitchen and looking out into the Great Room and seeing all these informal gatherings of conversation... Colleagues on the long benches, gathered around the harvest table, looking through the open French doors hearing their laughter around patio tables... the sun streaming through the windows. It just made me happy!"

Though her Peace Corps assignment in Zambia ended early, she took from that experience a sense of the critical importance of education and a new volunteer assignment in Boston schools. Her compelling focus has been the unique needs in special education, a focus gained from experiences teaching at the elementary school, middle school, and now at Shorewood High School outside Seattle. To heighten her skills, she earned a Masters in Special Education from Texas A&M and is now studying for a Doctorate of Education through Vanderbilt University. ❧

ABOVE The howling red metal wolf near the children's playhouse is our elusive attempt to warn the white-tail deer to stay away from plants.

wouldn't know most people in the room, and I'm usually drained by large groups. As a person of color, I'm usually asking myself, 'where are my allies and who will protect me?'"

She now comes back often, bringing other friends. "The Hearth feels so alive and it's so comfortable that I feel like I sit down and sink into the warmth. Every time I come I see something new, like the red tin coyote on the hillside, or being astonished at the size of the indoor Benjamina Ficus. And we have incredible conversations, including over very hard topics such as race relations. But we also just laugh a lot while here, and have such a sense we can just be ourselves."

Colleagues Maren Hayes and Michael Marchesini met briefly in their cohort class at the Hearth. Then Michael traveled to Nicaragua with Jesuit Volunteers and worked with microfinance groups while Maren moved to Tucson with Presbyterian Year in Mission serving border-crossers in a sanctuary church. Two years later, they returned and attended a Debriefing Conference at the Hearth.

Maren remembers the moment they began their friendship. "While relaxing one afternoon, Michael picked up the guitar and started playing 'Landlock Blues' and 'First Day of my Life', songs from Bright Eyes, an obscure band in the era." A music major, Maren knew the words and surprised him by singing along and drumming. She moved to Seattle for graduate school in Ethnomusicology where Michael also lived and they decided to gather other creative Krista Colleagues for a focus group around ideas in the book *The Artist's Way*. "It was during discussions around the book that our romance began," recalls Maren. Later, they expanded into a Spirituality group, inviting other Krista Colleagues desiring a community to explore the meanings and questions around living lives of faith.

"Most of us grew up in faith communities with traditional doctrinal expressions," said Maren. "But experiences and new knowledge in our twenties raised many questions and often caused estrangement. We longed to talk together where faith could be held with an open hand and a genuine spirit of inquiry, rather than where our questions were met with disapproval."

The group has met monthly for years, seeking to create community and rituals. As life events happen, with marriages, the birth of children, career moves, or graduate school, their candid conversations continue. Destiny Williams, a Colleague married to fellow Colleague Karolina Wright, finds the ongoing support and encouragement invaluable. "We have built enough trust that we can share our faiths and doubts, our humanness, and even build an accountability to one another as we consider how to walk in life together, to be there for each other."

Conversations of a broader nature began when several of our earliest Krista Colleagues wanted to expand our communication with other young

ABOVE A replica of an Irish Celtic cross sits above the Latin American courtyard. Krista Colleague Nathan Distelhorst, a talented saxophone player, wrote music for the dedication.

adult volunteers through the publication of *The Global Citizen, A Journal for Young Adults Engaging the World through Service*. They recognized that nothing similar existed for "twenty-somethings." Editor Aaron Ausland and Managing Editor Nathan Palpant worked with ten writers to produce the first edition.

They wanted to share specific experiences and reflections from those who are involved with global issues like poverty, race/culture/gender friction, and environmental stress. "The majority of our contributors are young Christian activists who have chosen a path of service for the love and hope of humanity and the planet," wrote Editor Aaron Ausland in the introduction. That's what prompted his essay, "Staying for Tea: Five Principles for the

ABOVE Aaron and Gabriela Ausland with our heart grandchildren, Ava London and Thiago, during a family reunion. Aaron served for a time as President of the Board.

Gabriela Ausland's Peanut Soup

Gabriela and Aaron created their own hearth of hospitality while living in Cambridge, MA, inviting many international students attending Harvard's Kennedy School with Aaron over for Bolivian Sunday suppers. Gabriela often made her mother's delicious and nutritious peanut soup recipe, similar to the one we serve at the Hearth.

Ingredients (for 8 people)
2 cups unsalted raw or roasted peanuts
2 quarts chicken broth or bouillon
1 big onion, chopped
4 potatoes, peeled and chopped into large chunks (as for a stew)
4 carrots chopped into small pieces
½ cup rice or quinoa
Salt, pepper, cumin to taste

Blend the peanuts in the blender. Next put the peanuts, chicken broth, onion, potatoes, carrots, salt, pepper, and cumin into a pot. Cook for 30 minutes. Add the rice or quinoa and cook for twenty minutes more. Top with garnishes of fresh chives, parsley, or green onions. If desired, chicken can be added for further protein.

Community Service Volunteer," a core reading for Krista Colleagues. This essay has also been utilized as a service-ethics tool in the curriculum of universities with international service programs, volunteer organizations that send out young adults, and church mission groups. Older citizens, who model a variety of ways of living lives of service leadership, contribute writings too. Their reflections offer wise insights on sustaining resilience amidst life's struggles.

The opposite of meaningful conversations is the silencing that represses difficult ones. Seeing how people visiting the Hearth found a space that inspired meaningful conversations, I decided to invite a group of mothers who had lost children to come for a weekend. Many experience America as a "grief-averse culture" that creates a silencing around the profound loss parents feel after the death of a child.

Too often, family and friends urge parents to "move on" after a short period of mourning. This inevitably leads to mothers and fathers being afraid to talk about the unsettling depth of ongoing grief. I also was seeking guidance and understanding from mothers who had walked this journey before our loss of Krista. For three days, mothers talked about how the death of their child broke their hearts and shattered their families. They also shared what resources gave them the strength and resilience to discover that life, though forever changed, can continue to unfold with meaning.

Each mother at the Hearth seemed energized and grateful for a chance to have conversations with each other on what it has been like to live with such heartbreaking loss. Their obvious joy of

ABOVE Feasting around the harvest table sparks many fascinating conversations as Krista Colleagues build friendships.

unbinding the silencing they felt encouraged me to interview other parents around the country on their grief journeys. These interviews eventually emerged in my book *Pilgrimage through Loss: Pathways to Strength and Renewal after the Death of a Child*. The book shows how some grieving parents found their lives continued to unfold with surprise connections of significance and delight.

The expansive friendships and meaning that have evolved through the work and wonder of the Krista Foundation and the Hearth and gardens have been unimaginable. For Aaron, his delight grew through meeting and marrying Gabriela, a beautiful Bolivian woman who volunteered with street children through MCC in Santa Cruz. They now cherish being parents of Thiago and Ava London. Gabriela is a bilingual educator in Seattle; Aaron

works globally for World Vision and designed the innovative program Youth Ready. Their children have become our heart-grandchildren, truly a gift to us. None of this changes the reality that we will miss Krista forever. But we live with gratitude for the community that has emerged as a legacy to her life.

The Kitchen and Dining Tables

Although the Hearth kitchen is small, the open floor plan links it to the Great Room with the long harvest table nearby. Knotted hickory cupboards and an antique red shelf add to the warmth of the marvelous aromas that waft from the carefully prepared meals. Whenever possible, we harvest fresh fruits and vegetables from the gardens, savoring a sun-ripened tomato or a bowl

"In a really difficult transition back from Central America, this home has been a safe and rejuvenating place. It's given me space for joy and mourning and important conversations and rest. What a gift!"

~Anna, Central America Study Tour 2018 that had to leave Nicaragua after violence erupted

ABOVE Our Latin American courtyard was inspired by visiting the many countries that create these places of intimate beauty as a central focus for hospitality.

of sweet raspberries and blueberries. Above the red ceramic sink is a village print of visual artist John August Swanson's global art. A Mexican artisan's painting on wood of San Pasqual, the patron saint of cooks and kitchens, adds folk charm.

A guest gave us the Scatter Kindness sign we placed above the kitchen entry. A dark brass bell created in Budapest rings Colleagues to a moment of gratitude for the abundance of a meal. We use the tile counters for serving wine and delicious buffet dinners. For Colleague meals, we try to use local fresh cuisine. Attention to different food needs

means many options are included for those desiring vegetarian and gluten-free recipes. Guests all help with food preparation and clean-up, which allows everyone to become a part of life at the Hearth. We want them to feel that it is theirs, that they are both host and guest.

LATIN AMERICAN COURTYARD

During warm days from May to October, the French doors in the Great Room flow out to the Latin American courtyard, another inviting

ANNIKA SCHAROSCH

For several years,
Colleagues attending
Debriefing Retreats came
to know Krista Colleague
Annika Scharosch and
her husband Jerry as volunteer cooks. She learned
her specialty, Paprika Chicken, volunteering in
post-communist Hungary. While there, she introduced high school students to concepts of democ-
racy and history. This allowed Annika to utilize
her Political Science and Peace Studies major from
Whitworth University in interesting ways.

Upon returning, she received the prestigious
Thomas More scholarship to Gonzaga Law School,
where recipients have demonstrated commitment
to public service. After clerking at Washington
State's Supreme Court, for the past ten years she
has practiced law with the Washington State
Attorney General's office, first at the Department of
Labor and Industry and now as General Counsel
for Eastern Washington University.

"We loved coming to the Hearth to cook," she
says, before the time commitments of raising three
young children took precedence. "It was always so
invigorating to hear younger Colleagues share their
stories, and their passion to serve others. We don't
live in circles where that's always a high priority.
They inspired us to want to go back out and make
a difference."

place for conversations. Over the years, as Jim
spent time in Latin America, he grew to love
the ways Latin Americans gathered in courtyard
spaces with family and friends. So we recreated
this at the Hearth.

An ice bucket filled with seltzers, beers, and
ice teas greets the new Krista Colleague cohort
class in May near the "Bienvenidos: mi casa es
tu casa" sign. A wicker settee and chairs with a
pottery chimera fireplace provide one gathering
place. Three outdoor dining tables seat up to 18
more guests. Branches from a maple tree hover

Winter Mulled Wine Recipe

Ingredients
1 bottle of red wine (burgundy,
    cabernet sauvignon, or merlot)
3 cups natural juices, not concentrate (spiced or natural
    apple cider without sugar, grape juice, or a mix of both)
2 sticks cinnamon
5 whole cloves placed in fresh orange and/or apple slices
3 star anise (if desired)
¼ cup honey
Juice of one orange, or cup of pineapple juice

Simmer, but do not boil, for at least an hour. Delicious aroma in
your home and warming to the spirits on a snowy winter night!

protectively over the staircase and lower patio and
offer shade. A St. Francis Talavera pottery statue
sits near a lime green lace-leaf Japanese maple that
accents the natural stone wall. Ceramic butterflies
and a wooden Quetzal bird adorn the cedar fencing
among the honeysuckle and climbing hydrangea
bushes.

Guests often help cook on the aging barbecue.
It's always a pleasure to hear the laughter as new
friendships are forming or old friendships are
being renewed. We sometimes bring in a bougain-
villea plant in memory of the magnificent ones
overflowing courtyards in sunnier climates. But
as annuals in Spokane, they look like miniature
imitations. However, golden rudebeckias, azaleas,
herbs, grasses, and hostas flourish.

Just up from the stone staircase sits a four-foot
Celtic cross, designed after one in ancient Ireland.
When surrounded by daffodils, it's a harbinger of

ABOVE Friends Marla and Luke Hyder and daughter Eliza enjoying a tea party on the patio. RIGHT Krista's high school friend, Kyle Bungee, built this children's playhouse from the old barn wood.

spring. Nathan Distelhorst, a Krista Colleague and fine saxophone player, led us in a hillside procession with his composition of an original song to dedicate the cross.

Above the patios sits a red children's playhouse created from the original barn wood. Edible grapes grow along the nearby split rail fence and a metal chicken from Mexico scratches in the barnyard dirt. A howling red tin coyote, crafted by a local artisan, provides our futile attempt to ward off the roaming deer. With a miniature picnic table, the playhouse offers one more welcome to children. ॐ

Chapter VII

A Blessing for Contemplation

"I thank You God for most this amazing day: for the leaping greenly spirits of trees and a blue true dream of sky; and for everything which is natural which is infinite which is yes."

~E.E. Cummings poem,
I Thank You God for This Amazing Day

OPPOSITE (counter clockwise from bottom) This replica of an ancient woman graces the small pond in the Asian garden. A perfect size pool where very young children go "fishing." One of several St. Francis statues that adds peace throughout the gardens.

For Contemplation:

May this Hearth and these gardens invite our contemplation and compel our commitment to stewardship of the earth, so wisely expressed in the 12th century by Hildegard of Bingen. A Benedictine abbess, considered the founder of scientific natural history in Germany, wrote:

Glance at the sun. See the moon and the stars.
Gaze at the beauty of earth's greenings.
Now, think.
What delight God gives to humankind
With all these things...
All nature is at the disposal of humankind.
We are to work with it. For
Without it, we cannot survive.

The term contemplation has acquired varied meanings, but it usually includes the action of looking thoughtfully at something for a long time. It is often considered a form of prayer or meditation for someone seeking to experience God. In the Christian contemplative tradition, the 6th century saint, Gregory the Great, summed up this meaning as the "knowledge of God that is impregnated with love." He referred to contemplation as "resting in God" and he saw this as God's gift that could lead to interior transformation.

When Hildegard says to "Gaze at the beauty of earth's greenings to see what delight God gives to humankind," she emphasizes the importance of paying close attention to the infinite beauty in our earth. This, she believes, will give us insight into God's all-generous love.

ABOVE RIGHT Krista Colleague Neshia Alaovae served with Jesuit Volunteers as a "Compassionate Companion" in a Washington D.C. hospice for formerly homeless people with end-stage HIV/AIDS. After completing her graduate studies and license in counseling, she opened a private practice as a psychotherapist with special emphasis for persons of color.

With stress dominating daily life, research on the health benefits of mindfulness infuses self-help literature. Scientific studies support its values. However, finding time for contemplation in our rushed techno-centric culture takes determined, almost radical, attention. It also helps to have spaces that lend themselves to pauses. So, especially in our gardens, we have intentionally created places for peace that invite one to rest. Adirondack chairs, swinging benches, large flat rocks, a hammock, and comfortable seating by the water all bid guests to unwind.

Mike Davis, a Krista Colleague working in urban Seattle, remembers well the healing effect of contemplative walking in the gardens one weekend. His younger brother, his cousin, and a friend had been murdered in his hometown of Kansas City. For three years, he traveled back and forth to be alongside his mom and several younger brothers and sisters during the shock of the deaths, the funerals, the murder investigation, the arraignment, and then the trial of the murderer. "As the oldest son, besides my personal devastation at losing my little brother, I felt a need to be a pillar for my family, and be engaged in their pain and grieving."

Shortly after the Kansas City trial, he came to the Hearth for a retreat. "I vividly remember going for a walk on the hillside and being so touched by the visual sense of peace. The trees, flowers, birds singing. I had no inner peace. But as I wandered to the pond, and heard the music of the waterfall and saw the serene beauty, I began to let the peace enter."

Later, Mike discovered the Secret Garden, and sat in the shade in the Adirondack chair and felt present to the moment. "Then I saw the sign 'You Can Trust Me, Love God.' It felt like when you are in a dark room and a small light illuminates it. It gave me a sense I could lean on God while in this dark grieving time of life. I wasn't alone."

At a deep level, he intuited the truth of the ancient words in Psalm 100:

"For God is sheer beauty
All generous in love,
Loyal always and ever."

He claims this as a subtle turning point towards the inner peace he craved as he sought to rebuild the broken parts of his family life.

Jim and I have also known the healing from grief that living on the land gives. Contemplation in a seasonal garden, from the chill stillness of winter, to the greening of spring, and the sun-kissed warmth of summer, offers a catchment to absorb the depth of life's swirling and complex emotions.

To the right of the stone staircase winding up to the Hearth, there's a three-tier rockery where we've created a remembrance of Krista. Under a pink weeping cherry, given to us from Whitworth University's English department, lies a natural granite stone engraved with the words "Krista Hunt Ausland, A Joy Forever."

One bleak November, Jim found a time of contemplation by Krista's memory garden gave rise to a poem he wrote called *A Season of Death*.

Cold, skeleton-like limbs spike the darkness.
Jet black days envelop dim walkway lights.
This is the season of death.

Crispy, prostrate brown leaves and twigs
Rustle across a cement patio.
Somber, dusky freshets plunge downward
Into an inky pool with soaked leaves.

Stairs arch upwards to the inscribed stone,
"Krista, A Joy Forever."
Her ashes strewn underneath chrysanthemums
And a Weeping Cherry.
I weep too. Desolation is so vast.

It's been six months since that bright spring morn
Turned stormy, gray and rainy
With arched rainbow pierced by lightning
Brought a huge hole in my heart.
I walk the season of death and embrace it:

The stick skeletons, the inky pool, the vast
*   darkness*
And a measured walk to the stone.
Her stone; beloved, even in death. I weep.

Writing his sorrow, spurred by times of resting and reflection by the pond, gave Jim a way to grieve.

ABOVE A stone memorial, inscribed with the words "A Joy Forever," honors Krista. It lies under a Weeping Cherry given to us from the English department at Whitworth University.

Contemplation within the Hearth also proves pivotal for some. One of our earliest Krista Colleagues, Mark Terrell, turned his compassion for the thousands of Spokane street kids into the founding of a downtown drop-in center, Cup of Cool Water. For many years he served as Executive Director, every day seeing the way young kids felt like "discards."

As a father himself, it tore him up to see children thrown out of their homes, or fleeing from profoundly hurtful family relationships. He knows their involvement as homeless teens places them in dangers that further damage their bodies and spirits. Building trusting relationships becomes a slow, often heart-rending mission. One season, when feeling especially burnt out, he came to the Hearth for a personal retreat. He describes a time of contemplation.

"I sat for a long time just meditating in front of the Montana Stone triptych, with the intricate beauty of the Trinity and Creation carved by the artist. Seeing the three tiny human figures on their journey along the pathway, somehow spoke to my own journey. Years of caring for street kids left me feeling vulnerable and fragile. I felt like I hadn't really been paying attention enough to my own journey, my authentic self and how God had made me. I thought I'd been paying attention to who I am within the vastness of God's love all these years. But now I wasn't so sure."

Although he had completed his Doctorate in Ministry a few years earlier, shortly after this time of contemplation he decided to enter further studies through a Spiritual Direction Academy in Oregon. "Taking time to pause that day, and pay attention to the troubling inner struggles proved so valuable." He now adds his skills as a spiritual director to the Cup of Cool Water staff who work the streets. "I know they struggle with burnout, a pain I understand so well."

Tucked under a roof eave at the top of the stairs leading to the bedrooms is an area just big enough for one comfortable meditation chair and a rattan side table. A Japanese print of a child contemplating the magnificence of Mount Fuji welcomes

BELOW AND RIGHT A chair in the Asian meditation nook lets guests look through the stained glass earth window created by Susan Kim, a leading Northwest artist.

one into this intimate space. Nearby a bed of multi-colored river stones holds an antique Chinese toy chest with a Bonsai arrangement. Here guests can bring a book, a cup of tea, and look out the stained glass window that anchors the space. The creator, Susan Kim, once a student of Spike Grosvenor, who designed our KF logo, is now a leading stained glass artist in Washington State. In this window, she circled the Western Hemisphere with rainbow colors and clear antique glass that invites guests to look out upon cedar and pine trees gracing the land.

This window is a "full circle" gift from Judi Gordon Bergen in memory of my only sibling, my brother Larry Christensen. Nominated for a Woodrow Wilson graduate scholarship to study in Europe, he had been saving funds earned as a Maître D' at Seattle's Space Needle restaurant when he was killed in a car accident. So my parents gave his post-college savings to Judi, a beloved family friend, for her senior year of college expenses.

When she heard we were creating the Hearth, she called from Toronto and said, "I want to return the amount from Larry's savings for a special gift. This way your brother becomes part of your family's remembrance of Krista too."

Most of the international art within the Hearth carries stories that resonate with our vision for young adults. Near the Asian meditation corner, a vibrant painting by an artist from Thailand shows the powerful perspective that shapes his exquisite drawings. The story goes that a young man was trained and immensely talented in classical Thai art that draws heavily from Buddhist and Hindu influences. Then as a young adult he converted to the Christian faith. However, the conservative leaders of their particular branch of Christendom insisted he could no longer practice his traditional art. In their theology, this form dishonored God.

ABOVE An artist from Thailand created the "Glory of God" painting featuring the Madonna and Child image. He merged his classical Buddhist and Hindu artistic traditions with his Christian faith.

Fortunately, he attended Chiang Mai University in Thailand. Professors in the art department in this private Christian college assured him that was a great misunderstanding about the possibilities within one's faith life. Instead, they encouraged him to utilize all his training and talented skills, but now to just "do it for the glory of God." Our print has classical Eastern images surrounding a Madonna and Child, his response to their reassurance. He called it "Glory to God."

ABOVE A stone pagoda in the spring Asian garden.

THE ASIAN GARDEN

Our son Jefferson, adopted from Korea, and his bride Kris wanted to do their rehearsal dinner at the Hearth, which gave us added incentive to complete the Asian garden. Just days before their celebration, we finished the waterfall and new pond, accented with a stone Asian lantern.

Each spring, this is the garden that first draws our eyes. Here it's easy to share E.E. Cummings's gratitude for the "leaping greenly spirits." Change happens daily! I am not an organized gardener who keeps an informative journal with records of where each plant goes. This means we often receive delightful surprises when plants emerge.

In snowy frigid winters, we know that this season of dormancy is actually alive with under-ground reinvigoration. The resurgence of new life finds us happily back in the garden, grateful for the assurance the seasons give. Once the danger of freezing passes, Jim turns on the pump for the hillside waterfall that circulates through our pond. The return of this gentle splashing brings music to our ears. Soon frog songs, actually quite loud in mating season, add their chorus.

The unfurling of the first ferns and white buds on our Star Magnolia announces that spring begins again. The light blue hepatica peep out, along with colorful crocus, miniature grape hyacinths, and hellebore Lenten roses, undaunted if snow still remains on the ground. Simultaneously, green shoots from the hundreds of daffodils, narcissus, crocus, hyacinth, hostas, and Lily of the Valley begin to dot the landscape. Once in bloom, their

"I didn't know there could be a place like this. It is what my soul has been hungering for! I want to move in!"

~Ann Yund

ABOVE Spokane is known as "the lilac city" and our gardens include pink, lavender, white, and grape colors that bloom with their enticing scent each spring.

fragrance and soft shades bring enchantment. Two blossoming forsythia open with yellow joy near a tall stone pagoda. White flowering trees bloom for weeks. "Hear blessings dropping their blossoms around you," a quote from 13th century Persian poet Rumi, happens literally before our eyes as pastel petals blanket the ground.

These irresistible shoots of hope emerge in Krista's memory garden too. Dainty blue forget-me-nots, white bleeding hearts, and cheery daffodils surround Krista's stone, with another Saint Francis blessing the space. We later discovered that the giant Chinese Ailanthus tree that hovers over Krista's garden goes by the common name "Tree of Heaven." All of these flowers burst into bloom just in time for our annual Day of Prayer on May 20th. Truly soul-saturating beauty.

ABOVE Children enjoy "fishing" in the smaller Asian garden rock pond.

In late spring, yellow Columbine dance near the pond, along with the start of purple Japanese water iris and a lavender Korean lilac. A replica of an ancient Chinese woman that we've nicknamed the "woman at the well" creates serenity near a tiny stone pond. This became a playful and safe "fishing pond" where our granddaughter Erin loved using magnetic poles to catch colorful tropical fish. Several varieties of yellow and pink Chinese Tree Peonies give dazzling elegance in May, a favorite bouquet for the Hearth. A delicate pink Kwanzan Cherry, similar to the swath of trees along the Potomac River in Washington D.C., blooms near a smaller weeping cherry in a garden planted in honor of my mother, Evelyn Christensen.

The peonies and cherry blossoms are followed by white, purple, and lavender lilacs that exude their exquisite scent along pathways. Spokane embraces her fame as the Lilac City, and all species truly flourish here. Variegated hostas emerge and their leaves enliven the shade gardens with hues of cream, green, and blue.

A kaleidoscope of elegant French tulips accentuates the blue door of the root cellar. For a few weeks multi-hued flowers on azaleas and rhododendrons enhance the landscape. However, compared to the giant lush species growing in the rainfall areas in Western Washington, our petite shrubs lack their robust glory. But a dramatic pink dogwood and tall drifts of Siberian Iris thrive here, giving pleasure to the many walkers on our lane.

We find the Asian garden conducive to contemplation, as well as renewal of friendships, laughter, and conversation. On the circular patios by the pond, guests relax under the hanging nightlights, often with world music in the background. Many flowers and vegetables grow in large Vietnamese ceramic pots, providing fresh produce for summer feasts.

We are never alone in the garden. Each spring, robins return to join the chickadees, juncos, nuthatches, and pine siskins that brighten the winter landscape. Soon serious nest building begins.

Nor is it always peaceful. Birds enter territorial fights at the feeders, and occasionally a small hawk dives onto the land, usually looking for moles, small squirrels, or mice. Flocks of turkeys, often with a dozen young ones, forage through the land leaving their dung as stepping hazards. Plus they scratch up newly planted seeds. One year I planted over two hundred sunflower seeds on a hillside and by summer only three plants had emerged. Clearly the rest had become food for our avian friends. What a humbling reminder that these creatures also call the garden home!

In late spring, the tiger swallowtail butterflies migrate from New Mexico or Baja California. As they float amidst the flower feast, sipping nectar from the lavender or zinnia, the splendor of their yellow and black wingspan shimmers in the sunlight. These ordinary creatures all seem to shout of our Creator's imaginative and extraordinary genius.

One day amidst container plants on the patio, a friend and I spent a half hour observing a neon green praying mantis. We watched this distinctive insect swivel its triangular head a full 180 degrees, while its elongated front legs remained in a prayer position while waiting to snatch their dinner. It's not surprising that some early civilizations thought the praying mantis had supernatural powers.

RIGHT Tiger swallowtail butterflies, praying mantis, and a hummingbird nest add to the surprises discovered each day in the gardens.

RACHEL NOVAK

Rachael Novak, now the Climate Science Coordinator for the Bureau of Indian Affairs in the Department of the Interior, began her Krista Colleague journey when she was an AmeriCorps Volunteer as the environmental educator for the South Santiam Watershed Council in Sweet Home, Oregon. An environmental science major from Oregon State University and a member of the Navajo Nation, she later moved back to Arizona.

She wanted to pursue her interest in climate change impacts on the Navajo reservation through a master's degree in geosciences at the University of Arizona. She interviewed elders in the tribe to record their memories of how weather and climate impacted family farms and sheep raising. This led to her thesis on the intersection of traditional knowledge and climate science. When her baby was born, she also drew on the Navajo tradition of creating a celebration for simple wonders of the world, including a baby's first laugh.

She moved to Washington D.C. in 2008 to work for the Environmental Protection Agency (EPA) as a physical scientist on water quality as part of America's Clean Water Act. Her work now focuses on helping tribes with climate adaptation planning in order to be more resilient to climate change impacts. She married early in 2017 and was blessed with a son recently. She hopes all of her work contributes to helping protect Nahasdzáán Shimá (Mother Earth) for her son and future generations. ॐ

Scientists recently discovered they actually have unique 3-D vision and are studying them to develop vision in robots. A miraculous tiny creature.

Twice a year we bring in a local company, Spirit Pruners, to help shape our larger trees. Their staff shares the belief that attentiveness to nature proves essential. We saw this in action one afternoon while a gardener was thinning our high Chokecherry tree.

"I was just starting to prune when I heard a bird clearly in distress," he told us. "Looking up, I saw above me a frantic mother hummingbird. I instantly stopped cutting the branch and then saw the teeniest of bird's nests with two baby hummingbirds."

This is a rare sighting because their nests are amazingly camouflaged, often resembling a small knot on a tree limb. So tiny and so perfect, some ornithologists consider them one of the wonders of the earth. For five to seven days, the mother hummingbird searches for nesting materials, often taking up to 34 trips per hour for four hours a day. Our gardens offer a smorgasboard for a hummingbird's favored soft fibers. Silken hairs, fuzzy seedpods, moss, lichen, cottonwood, pasque flowers, clematis, honeysuckle and the plumes of oriental grasses all help create the spongy cradle for her babies.

The mother bird constructs a velvety compact cup, about the size of a walnut shell. She binds cotton fluffs, bits of willow, twigs, leaves, and plant fibers with spider web silk. To protect from predators, she chooses branches high up a tree, and finds shelter under leaves to keep her babies from being blown out by strong winds. The jellybean size eggs incubate for 15 to 18 days, and fledglings stay in their nest for another 18 to 28 days after hatching. Most interesting, the elastic sides stretch as babies grow. We were thankful our grandchildren happened to be visiting from Boston and could enjoy our daily watch of this natural marvel.

ABOVE Calypso Borealis plant, akin to the one environmentalist John Muir discovered that electrified his sense of wonder. Muir's writing as a botanist inspires Jim's interest in plants and gardens. .

Muir wrote,

> I found beautiful Calypso on the mossy bank of a stream, growing not in the ground but on a bed of yellow mosses in which its small white bulb had found a soft nest and from which its one leaf and one flower sprung. The flower was white and made the impression of utmost simple purity like a snow flower. No other bloom was near it, for the bog a short distance below the surface was still frozen, and the water was ice cold. It seemed the most spiritual of all the flower people I had ever met. I sat down beside it and fairly cried for joy.

Muir's description introduced Jim to the power of full attentiveness to our natural world and led Jim to write *Restless Fires: Young John Muir's 1000 mile Walk to the Gulf in 1867-68*. Muir has become a touchstone for Jim's appreciation of all that grows here.

Although we have strong gardeners who help at least once or twice a week in season, Jim and I work alongside them to help plant, prune, transplant, weed, and attend to the pond. It's a lot of work, but it keeps us open to the garden's wonders. It might be seeing a covey of quail with their little ones skittering across the lawn, or the scent of the Spokane lilac while climbing the stone stairs, or a baby fawn still bearing white spots. Hearing him say "Linda, come see!" always intrigues me. Like Muir, Jim now also keeps a daily journal of gratitude, increasing his awareness of all he sees on the land and in life.

In the midst of working in the gardens, we discover new gifts come each day. I've never quite understood the intellectual resistance to miracles recorded in the Biblical accounts. Isn't the planting of a nondescript brown seed that emerges in the grand splendor of a towering sunflower or a heritage tomato plant its own miracle? Or seeing a mottled bulb gradually

For years, Jim has been influenced in his care for our gardens by his research on America's leading early environmentalist John Muir. The founder of the Sierra Club, Muir's lifelong study of botany and passion for the earth inspired the establishment of our national parks system. His writings exude a sense of wonder and overwhelming gratitude for the Creator and for creation. He clearly understood Hildegard's urging nine centuries earlier regarding nature, that we "must work with it, for without it we can't survive." As Muir's influential quote says, "All things are hitched together." These concepts shape Jim's own gratitude of the daily wonders in our Hearth gardens. One of Muir's earliest writings describes a Canadian botanizing adventure looking for the rare Calypso Borealis orchid.

"I have truly loved sitting outside in the garden with my daughter within the beauty of your plantings among God's creatures. We have chuckled at the antics of the squirrels and sighed over the beauty of the hummingbirds. We even saw a deer!"

~Krista guest

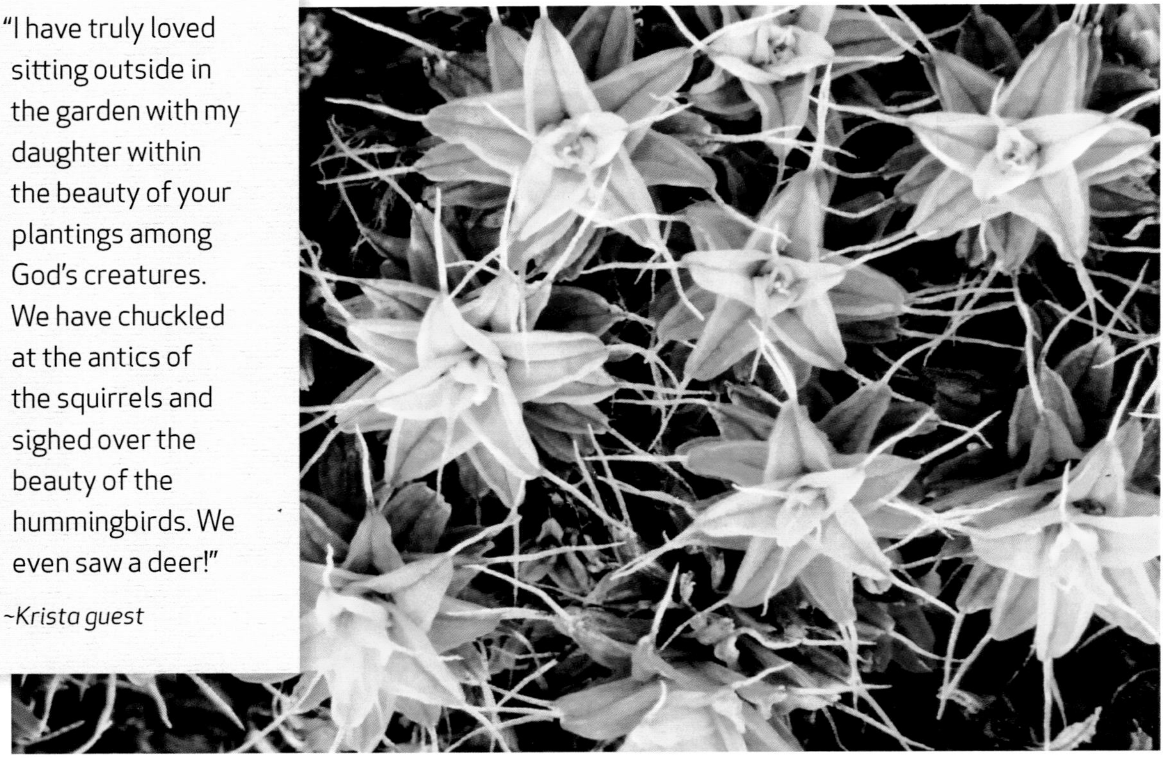

ABOVE Magnified photograph by Larry Daloz of one the many distinctive mosses in the Northwest, including the Hearth gardens. Larry finds, "There's a healing power of astonishment when seeing the beauty of these exquisite plants so often ignored."

emerge into a dramatic Café au Lait Dinner Plate Dahlia or a stunning Stargazer Oriental Lily also a kind of genetic miracle?

Even after years in our gardens, we are acutely aware of how much more exists that we barely notice. When Larry Daloz, longtime friend, environmental activist, and bryophyte phographer, visited, he became fascinated with our rich variety of mosses. He spent hours focusing his camera lens on their intricacies, including a three-inch Coscinodon calyptratus discovered on our terraced garden. "I love the extraordinary beauty of mosses and how fast they shift and change," he told us. "One minute they dazzle as moisture expands; then they might shrivel and almost disappear. Even in just five minutes of time. It's magical. They remind me to seek being present and alive each moment to the miracles in life!" His observations remind us to keep attentive to our own small gift of land, always full of surprising treasures.

From its inception, the Krista Foundation Board understood that care for the environment ranks as one of the defining challenges of our times. So, when the cohort class of Krista Colleagues is selected each year, one of the three categories we support includes young adults who give their energy and skills within environmental service. Our hope is that for all Colleagues and guests visiting the gardens, the contemplation of life's amazing natural world inspires a deep desire to care for the earth, our beloved planet home.

ABOVE Drs. Larry Daloz and Sharon Parks during an exhibit of his bryophyte moss photography at the Whidbey Arts gallery.

JESSICA ZIMMERLE

When Jessica Zimmerle was serving with Earth Ministry in Seattle through Lutheran Volunteer Corps, she utilized her $1000 Krista Colleague Service Leadership grant to attend a major conference. New York Theological Seminary sponsored an international program, Religion for the Earth. "To see persons from around the world showing their passion and professional concern for care of our earth really expanded my vision," recalls Jessica. "I began to sense that faith-based environmental work was my life calling."

While at the Hearth for a Debriefing Retreat, she had been pondering going to seminary to ground her environmental commitments with a deeper theological awareness. But she was hesitant. "I was journaling quietly with Colleagues at the harvest table, a place I love. I gained a heart clarity that day, deciding to take the leap and enroll."

Jessica now attends Seattle University School of Theology and Ministry while continuing at Earth Ministry, but in a staff position as the Program and Outreach Director. "My dream is that one day church members will see care for creation as central as care for the poor since they are so related."

Chapter VIII

A Blessing for Compassion

*"Love and compassion are necessities,
not luxuries. Without them,
humanity cannot survive."*

~The Dalai Lama

LEFT A tin creation of Our Lady of Guadalupe, an image of compassion
venerated in Mexico, hangs near the Latin American room door.

For Compassion:

May renewal at the Hearth enliven our spirit of compassion, growing as global citizens. Encourage our desire to practice the spirit of loving-kindness in our daily lives: to ourselves, our families, our communities, all creatures great and small, and our planet home.

Compassion is often described as "empathy in action." It includes a sympathetic consciousness of others' distress, together with a desire to help alleviate and prevent it, to somehow mitigate that pain and suffering.

The first step towards enlivening compassion usually involves awareness, what Aaron Ausland refers to in his writings on global citizenship as "expanding our circle of empathy." Because of Krista's expressed desire to "show God's love in actions," one criteria for the selection of Krista Colleagues is that they serve within an organization that gives opportunities for direct hands-on service. After a Krista Colleague spends a year helping AIDS patients dying in a Hospice House, or provides endangered turtles with reproduction protection in their ravaged habitats, or assists differently abled adults living in a L'Arche home, their compassionate awareness of life challenges is vastly enhanced.

During Debriefing Retreats, 10 to 15 Colleagues spend extended days at the Hearth, and share stories. For many Colleagues, living close to those facing stark daily struggles forever changes their insight and understanding. Their own global awareness further expands as they listen to each other. One Colleague may illustrate the needs of first generation immigrant children in urban Tacoma, Washington, while another may share her insights into the barriers for women seeking to leave the sex-trade industry in Ethiopia, or another may show how the development of a community garden in a food wasteland in urban America offers both healthy meals and companionship. When hearing each other's stories they clearly value discovering powerful common threads. These shared understandings of the joys and struggles of their service journeys can be hard to find among their peers.

Shortly after we opened the Hearth, we saw how this space creates room for lively compassion for other guests too. One afternoon, we received a call asking if the Hearth could be available for a family from Texas whose daughter, Cameron, was killed the previous night near the Whitworth University campus. A major sporting event in the city meant every hotel room was filled. "Of course," we said, in wonderment that one of the first uses of the Hearth was for another family needing comfort after losing a daughter.

So Jan and Harold Skaggs flew in from Texas with their son and stayed for a few days. For Jan, her own earlier experiences of the importance and power of forgiveness shaped her attitude toward the young man who killed their daughter. "It was a dark and rainy night and Cameron was wearing dark clothes. The driver had just left the fire station where he was training in EMT. He had a green light to turn; she had the 'go' to walk. But the light was out at the crosswalk and he never saw her." The Skaggs heard how traumatized the young man was, and that he had tried in vain to save her. They knew he was blaming himself. "He took her death seriously, which we appreciated, and we heard he felt very guilty."

Though reeling with their own pain, they chose to invite him to come to the Hearth to meet them. "We wanted him to know we were not holding this against him and that we forgave him. At first, his fire department mentor was hesitant to have him come because he assumed we'd want to lash out at him. He finally understood we wanted to communicate a spirit of forgiveness."

When he arrived at the Hearth door, the Skaggs welcomed him with a hug, but he could barely look at them. As they talked, sitting around the fireplace, Jan told him, "We know this was an accident and that you'd do anything to take it back if you could." She also encouraged him to get counseling along with his young wife. "You will be forever changed, but we want you to get help and go forward in life. Otherwise your own mother will also lose a child. Please know that we forgive you."

A police investigator stood in the back of the Hearth observing the Skaggs' words of generous forgiveness. Later he told us, "In all my years of working with accidents, I've never seen anything like this." Jan knew there is freedom in forgiveness, not just to the one forgiven, but for herself. She entered into the suffering of a young man and his mother, offering her heart of compassion.

"What a blessing, and a wonderful, tangible remembrance of your daughter. The whole building radiates peace, a real unique feeling these days. It inspires me to want to be kinder, more thoughtful and more intentionally a bearer of peace."
~ *Sarah Brody, guest*

We were immensely grateful there was "no room in the inn" at local motels. It was hard to imagine this level of communication in a one-bedroom motel room, and certainly not in a public lobby. Later, I saw Harold, clearly exhausted, lying asleep on the couch. He offered a poignant sign fulfilling our hope that a relaxed-looking sofa might encourage a resting spirit. The Skaggs' actions gave us an early glimpse of how the Hearth space allows loving-kindness to be kindled and practiced.

From the beginning, we sought to be an intergenerational community. We wanted older adults who exemplify lifelong leadership to offer their wise insights. One year, Jesuit Father Greg Boyle, founder of Homeboy Industries, shared his life with our community. Author of *Tattoos on the Heart*, Father Boyle is renowned for his innovative approach to intervention and rehabilitation with gangs in East Los Angeles. Very tough work. He expanded our understanding of compassion when he encouraged Colleagues to recognize that "the truest compassion does not come from wanting to help out those less fortunate than ourselves or on the margins. Instead, we need to be willing to see ourselves in kinship with them."

This idea of kinship parallels a core principle that centers our service-ethics preparation for Krista Colleagues. As mentioned earlier, we introduce the concept of "Staying for Tea" through an essay that emerged from Aaron and Krista's experience in accompaniment while in Bañado de la Cruz. New Colleagues read this in preparation for their first cohort gathering at the Hearth and our Memorial Day retreat. The essay, published in our *Global Citizen Journal*, is used by many other organizations such as universities, church mission groups, and young adult service agencies to also prepare their communities in service ethics.

With the major struggles of our era, some Colleagues find that compassion includes working intently for structural change. Whether participating in matters of racial and social justice, immigration and refugee inequities, criminal justice reform, economic and educational disparity, gender concerns, or climate change, there are Colleagues actively engaged in efforts to create a more just world.

Whether running for political office, using law degrees for citizen rights, writing books on ethics, building entrepreneurial businesses, creating loving homes and neighborhoods, pursuing Ph.D.s in Special Education, engaging in medical research and practice, or contributing to the Environmental Protection Agency, they are finding ways of being compassionate citizen leaders at the local and international level.

Our hope is that the kinship emerging while listening respectfully and attentively within one's service experience ultimately translates into Colleagues' future civic leadership in our nation.

Self-Compassion

The Buddha is believed to have said, "If your compassion does not include yourself, it is incomplete."

The Hearth also offers a place for guests to practice loving kindness to themselves. We wanted a genuine place of respite and refreshment for guests. Since nominated Colleagues tend to be recognized high achievers, one of the shadow sides for some is a critical inner voice as they set such high standards for themselves. The almost overwhelming burdens they see people carry can also cause some to slip into feeling they are never doing enough. This is especially true if they compare themselves to other talented and motivated persons.

To live a lifelong ethic of service we encourage practicing the art of balancing action with contemplation and learning. Research shows that compassion fatigue and burnout are real concerns, especially for those engaged in the helping professions. Just having a few days of good rest, relaxing in a peaceful garden, finding private moments to journal, or laughter and conversation over healthy meals proves restorative.

In describing the Hearth table to new Krista Colleagues in his *Global Citizen* essay "Come to the Table," Aaron invites them to enjoy "this table of celebration, bounty, thanksgiving, hospitality, rest, and wonder. Around it you'll find invigorating conversations, curious sampling of new foods and culture, grateful spirits and cries of 'pull up a chair and make yourself at home...mi casa es tu casa!'"

He encourages Colleagues to find these moments of enjoyment to keep a healthy perspective. "At the Hearth table, we step away momentarily from the suffering and pain in communities where we serve. We don't forget it, but we recognize that this is not all there is in the world. This is also a place of beauty, kindness and provision. We step away also to remember to not take ourselves so seriously." Learning to care for ourselves if we want to help others echo's Christ's wisdom "to love our neighbor as ourselves."

Receiving Compassion

Jim often shares with Colleagues at the Hearth the story behind Quechua Dama, a poem he wrote that is published in the *Global Citizen Journal*. It illustrates the transformative possibilities when we are open to receiving compassion that comes to us.

A few years after Krista's death, Jim was returning from Machu Picchu in Peru. He missed Krista intensely as he relived memories of their adventures traveling together in Latin America. Climbing on the local bus, he received a much needed gift when his sorrow-filled heart connected to the generous spirit of a Quechua woman. He experienced the universal power and kinship of sharing bread together, reminiscent of the Christian liturgical practice of communion.

As Jim discovered during this transformative moment of grace, receiving compassion from others enriches our days. He encourages Colleagues to have hearts attentive to all the good gifts they receive from others while in service. This will strengthen their own capacity to give compassion.

QUECHUA DAMA
by Jim Hunt

Hustled from train to bus
There, next to her, an empty seat.
She nodded approval of my occupying its
Emptiness.
Her stout frame amply filled the seat's corner

I, long, white and lank
Appeared as if from a different world.
Brown hat, sunglasses, blue eyes, white skin.
She, dark, short, hair tinged with grey,
teeth missing.
Still, she smiled and nodded.

We chatted in Spanish about
Houses, trees, mountains, and families.
As the bus lurched along
Our generalities became specifics.

I, a daughter died three years ago.
She, a daughter too, in a bus accident.
Both, in magical ways were twenty-five.
Our eyes locked, both brimming with tears.

I choked mine back.
But she, lady that she was
Dove deep into her blue plastic shopping bag
And lifted high beautiful Peruvian pan.

She broke it and offered me some.

A BLESSING OF THE HEARTH QUILT

by Jim Hunt

For the sun and rain and earth that
    Produced the crops for cotton and dyes
Our Creator God, we thank you.

For the farmers who tilled the land,
    nurtured and harvested the crops
Our Creator God, we thank you.

For the artisans and designers who
    created the colors,
Wove the fabric, and pieced and
threaded the shapes
Our Creator God, we thank you.

For the families who brought the fabrics
    to the marketplace
And the vendors who brought them
    to our land
Our Creator God, we thank you.

For Kathleen Hume's skill as a seamstress,
    her passion and talents with cloth
Our Creator God, we thank you.

For her servant's spirit, her love of Christ,
    her heartfelt memories of Krista, and
    her tangible hands-on encouragement to
    the vision of the Krista Foundation
Our Creator God, we thank you!

ABOVE This large quilt of the Krista Foundation logo was created by neighbor Kathleen Hume and enlivens the staircase wall. She used international fabrics from countries where Krista Colleagues volunteered.

The Hearth has also received acts of compassionate kindness. Our next-door neighbor, Kathleen Hume, knew Krista since childhood, and grieved her death with us. So when we built the Hearth, she wanted to share her immense talent as a seamstress and quilter. She offered to make a quilt with the Krista Foundation logo in the center using fabrics from countries where Colleagues served.

For a few months, we collected fabrics imported from around the world, and then she wove her magic. The quilt hangs on the stairway wall, plus we often take it to fundraising events where it enlivens the speaker's podium and conveys the warmth and beauty of the Hearth. On June 15, 2006, we dedicated it with a blessing. It's a tangible symbol of the compassionate gifts we all receive each day from friendships, from artisans, from the earth, and from our Creator.

THE LATIN AMERICAN ROOM

Almost like being perched in a treehouse, the small Latin American room overlooks the waterfall and gardens. By sliding open the window, guests hear the musical sounds of water tumbling down a hillside of moss-covered rocks. A striking tiered maple arches over the pond where birds flit by to bathe on Spokane's sun-drenched days. Ferns unfurl in the nearby woodland garden amidst white Lily of the Valley, and the perfume scent of purple, white, and lavender lilacs infuse the pathways.

It's a productive space for many who come to the Hearth, especially those wanting to focus on a particular project. Near natural beauty, the room allows for focused concentration, often hard to find. A furniture craftswoman built a desk from reclaimed wood accented by iron butterflies, which holds a computer, printer, and reference books. It's here that Krista Colleagues and friends have developed the first *Global Citizen Journal*, planned our annual Memorial Day conference materials, designed weddings and showers, filled out applications for graduate studies, prepared public presentations and speeches, and written essays. I found it immensely helpful for focused concentration while finishing my book for grieving families *Pilgrimage through Loss*. Whatever tasks benefit from stillness and distance from distractions are enhanced here.

When Krista was an exchange student in Guatemala City, her host family taught her their art of weaving pictures. Her efforts show two traditionally dressed women in colorful clothing selling flowers. It hangs by the doorway near a Mexican tin

ABOVE (left) In the Latin American room and library, the couches become hide-a-beds for overnight guests. (right) When Krista was 16, she lived one summer as an exchange student with a Guatemalan family who taught her their wool embroidery craft form. She created this picture of traditionally dressed women that hangs near the Latin American room.

ABOVE Krista Colleagues often find the Latin American room offers a quiet place to journal, write essays, applications to graduate school, or job resumes. A craftswoman used reclaimed wood and iron butterflies to create the desk

artist's creation of the revered Lady of Guadalupe. More weavings, folk dolls, pottery, and paintings enhance a sense of the abounding artistic spirit and talent of Latin American artists.

My favorite painting is a charming Nicaraguan village wedding scene that reminds me of the primitivist paintings from the Solentiname archipelago in Nicaragua. It was in these alluring but desperately poor islands that poet-priest Ernesto Cardenal discovered the artistic originality of the people. In the 1960s, he brought attention to the island painters from global art collectors who found themselves captivated by the idealized rainforests and blue-green watery scenes. This generated the first reliable income for artists who continue to sell their sought-after work. These distinctive acrylic and oil paintings, often populated by white egrets, blue herons, and blackbirds, sometimes even hang on embassy walls around the world.

The success of the Solentiname artists spurred other painters throughout Nicaragua to use their talent to earn a livelihood. Our picture came from a Nicaraguan market artist, but exudes the same joie de vivre. A bride and groom emerge from the white chapel, accented by the brilliant blue ocean, red and green palm trees, and stucco and tile buildings. A farmer with his oxen, a driver in a red car, street dogs, men, women, children, and an outdoor market stall reflects the diversity of human activity still found in most Latin American villages. It brings back fond memories to most of our Colleagues who served in Latin America and found such villages vibrant with life.

ABOVE The hand carved Tree of Life coat hanger comes from a Bolivian market.

Two beautiful jackets made by talented weavers from Cochabamba are displayed on a hand-carved Tree of Life from Bolivia. Made from Aguayo weavings originally created by indigenous mothers to carry their babies, they remind us of Krista's days of coming to know and love women in her remote river valley of Bañado de la Cruz.

CREATURES ON THE LAND

Every home on the lane where we live has acreage that goes up one or two acres to the fertile Five Mile Prairie. The basalt rock and natural habitat becomes a protected corridor for wild life. So when guests walk the land, it's possible to enjoy all creatures great and small. Even more, we hope that experiencing this joy might inspire acts of care and compassion towards all creation.

Depending on the season, one might see a wild brown or red rabbit, an occasional raccoon, marmot or skunk, or be warned of cougar sightings. Almost daily we see families of white-tailed deer, a covey of quail, sometimes with teeny baby chicks, and grey squirrels. At night, one can even hear the howling from a distant den of coyotes.

NISSANA NOV REVET
After completing her AmeriCorps experience, it was the open conversations at the Krista Colleague Debriefing Retreat that Nissana Nov Revet remembers vividly.

"We were mostly strangers to one another when we began. Yet, as we shared our stories, there was a spirit of openness and vulnerability, with lots of laughter and tears. Now many are lifelong friends, and I've loved seeing how they have evolved and grown," said Nissana. She especially enjoyed the meals and conversations around the table. "These times taught me this is the kind of spirit I want to have in my home when I start a family. Of course, the wine and chocolate helped!"

Nissana continued her interest in immigrants and refugees while earning a Master's Degree in Social Work at Columbia University where she focused on social enterprise administration and working with children in the Bronx. She also comes from a Cambodian refugee family of traditional dancers where she learned the importance of keeping one's culture alive. "I saw my mother's commitment to teaching Tacoma, Washington's Cambodian children the beauty of their dances."

Conversations continue to be central in Nissana's co-owned consulting practice D-Fine Concepts. Their focus on equity provides support to city and county government agencies needing to bring marginalized voices, especially immigrants, youth, and the elderly, into the public sphere.

KARA KING

Kara King saw the impact of family abuse and trauma and the healing power of a loving community through her years of working with Nuestros Pequeños Hermanos (NPH) orphanages in Latin America, first as a volunteer and later as a staff leader in El Salvador, Honduras, and Bolivia. When she returned to Seattle to teach second grade, she initiated a new NPH program.

Each year, a select group of NPH graduates come to America to learn English and leadership skills. One Christmas, they stayed at the Hearth and gave us a painted pottery shard in the shape of Bolivia, symbolizing "once they were broken, and now are whole."

Kara's spirit of compassion led her into a career shift. She attended the Seattle School of Theology and Psychology to earn her Masters in Counseling. When she opened her office to begin her private counseling practice, she remembered the story of prayers in the Hearth foundation. "Since my specialty is for persons in trauma and abuse, I wanted God's spirit in this space. So I wrote prayers above the baseboards before painting over them. Clients need to face very hard life experiences, and need a sense of peace, safety, and protection. My own Hearth place!"

Always there are surprises. One sunny afternoon, while enjoying tea in the Latin American patio with Hearth guests, we saw a squirrel skittering across the top rung of the Latin American courtyard fence. Nothing unusual about this. But soon after, three tiny baby squirrels, usually very elusive, followed behind their mama. A rare sighting, our first in the years we've lived here!

When we bought this home and land, it was clear earlier owners enjoyed gardening, both for beauty and for the provision of food they stored in the handbuilt root cellar. Their efforts gave us an abundant plant heritage, including the prominent Tree of Heaven. Now sixty years later, as we prepared the land to build the Hearth, a large branch was hugging a nearby ponderosa pine.

Our contractor recommended we take down the pine.

Hesitant to remove the stately tree, we asked a respected Spokane tree arborist to guide our decision. As he surveyed the connections between the two trees and considered their root systems, he advised us, "They've got a special relationship and have worked it out. Don't disturb it!" Given the growing understanding of forest life today, this makes sense. We kept the glorious 40-foot pine. The trees still hug.

Creating an environment where creatures thrive adds daily satisfaction. During the deepest years of sorrow after Krista's death, Jim found solace by faithfully filling the bird feeders, especially through the harsh winter. He continues to provide a variety of choices, including white and red millet, whole black-oil sunflower seeds, and sunflower hearts and nectar. His efforts attract a delightful community of birds. Nuthatches, chickadees, juncos, California quail, tiny sparrows, robins, pine siskins, and hummingbirds call the Hearth their home too. Now and then a towhee, Baltimore Oriole, or owl will make an unexpected appearance.

At the pond and waterfall we're used to seeing all of these birds, but one morning Jim was aston-

ished by a visitor. "I was filling the birdfeeders when a Great Blue Heron swooped down towards the pond, likely eyeing the goldfish. It paused on the roof of the Hearth across from me and eyed me intently. It seemed to be saying, 'you are in the way of my breakfast.'" Fascinated, Jim stayed very still to watch it. Eventually the heron gave up, spread his magnificent five-foot wingspan, and lifted off.

On a much tinier scale, by placing the favored feed of thistle and nyger seed, we've now been able to draw pairs of the brilliant yellow goldfinches. Their presence gives guests at the Hearth a dramatic glimpse of Washington State's bird.

The hummingbirds benefit from our succession plantings and are especially attracted to red, a common color in their feeders. In Eastern Washington, we primarily see the Rufous hummingbird, Anna's hummingbird, and Calliope. We've enjoyed having children observe intently from the patio and be entertained with their helicopter flying skills. To augment the feeders, we've added tubular shaped flowers like foxgloves, coral bells, zinnias, delphinium, honeysuckle, and trumpet vine that allow the humming-birds to feed with their long beaks.

From the beginning, we've also been planting to attract bees and butterflies. Especially with the colony collapse disorder and mysterious die-off of honeybees in North America, bee friendly plantings by backyard gardeners could help these distressed pollina-tors. Bees primarily need nectar that is loaded with sugar and provides their main source of energy, plus pollen that gives them a balanced diet of proteins and fats.

Yet many hybridized plants that gardeners appreciate, especially for improved disease resistance, flower size, and color, have reduced

"This is a place in which human dignity flourishes. And the earth itself!"

~Michael Barram, guest

JOE TOBIASON

 Serving in Lima, Peru, with the Joining Hands network meant that Joe Tobiason often took American delegations up into the Andes. "This is when my passion for photography began. I wanted chances to talk with Peruvians and dig into their culture," said Joe, a Cross-Cultural Studies major fluent in Spanish. "The camera became the vehicle that gave me a wonderful opportunity to hear their stories."

For years he's worked honing his craft in people-based photography and building his Seattle business, JTobiason Photography, primarily as a wedding photographer. "I want to make joyful photography, and wedding celebrations really lend themselves to creating lifetime memories. Each family has a culture that I try to understand so I capture what's important to them." He drew on these similar skills when Heifer International sent him to Bangladesh and Peru to portray their story.

It's the calmness the Hearth gives that is vividly etched in his memory. "When I first came back from Peru, I was struggling to find work and found myself worried and depressed. A friend and I stayed at the Hearth for a couple of days and I felt its calming peace. By the time we left, my spirits felt far stronger!"

or completely eliminated their pollen and nectar. So mixing in heirloom plants and native plants in our gardens, plus flowers and shrubs that bloom throughout the seasons, assures a food supply. A perennial row of lavender goes up our long driveway and draws hundreds of bees throughout spring and summer; then clusters of asters bloom nearby until frost in the fall.

Bees have good color vision and are attracted to the bright flowers in blue, red, purple, violet, white, and yellows. Interspersed in the gardens are blue salvia, rudbeckia daisies, coneflowers, nasturtiums, candytuft, sweet alyssum, and columbine, all often abuzz with honeybees.

Butterflies graze on these same plants, but they also want places where they can momentarily rest like on our quince and cotoneaster shrubs and our flowering dogwood. Our patio herbal gardens, with rosemary, basil, thyme, and marjoram, are another draw. We try to minimize use of any pesticides since this will harm these cherished creatures. When guests wander in the gardens, they experience how this land nourishes vibrant life all around them.

Environmental stewardship reigns as one of the most pressing global issues of our era. Krista, like others in the younger generations, sensed this keenly. So when we established the Krista Foundation, one of the three criteria for potential Krista Colleagues included those going into environmental service. Our Colleagues have served in the United States and around the world with environmental projects through organizations such as the Peace Corps, AmeriCorps, Earth Ministry, EarthCorp, and smaller community-based grassroots efforts. As they seek solutions to the perils facing our planet, these volunteer experiences shape their awareness of the further skills needed to be compassionate environmental stewards. For some, this launched their desire for environmental careers and further graduate school training, and they now serve as staff members of environmental organizations. ໑

RIGHT Coveys of California quail, Calliope, and Anna hummingbirds. We love to see the vibrant Washington State bird, the Goldfinch, nest on the Hearth lands.

Chapter IX

A Blessing for Confidence and Courage

"The birds they sang at the break of day.
Begin again, I heard them say...
Ring the bells that still can ring
Forget your perfect offering
There is a crack in everything
That's how the light gets in."

~Leonard Cohen, Anthem

LEFT Giant spruce, fir, and pine trees surround the gardens and first attracted us to this land. Many are nearly 100 years old or more.

"I am still devoted to the garden"

Thomas Jefferson

For Confidence and Courage:

Let us leave the Hearth infused with Thy Spirit, confident in Jesus's promise that we are not alone. In a world that hungers for peace, use the gatherings in this space to help us walk humbly on this earth, but with abundant belief that we are to "Be strong and of good courage, for I will be with you."

For most people, there are places of the heart where we find a greater calmness, a freedom to be ourselves, and a restored confidence when we leave to "start again" with more courage for that which challenges us. When we traveled to North Carolina for a sabbatical, we heard Southerners refer to these as "peace-bringin'" places.

Often these are places we discover in nature. In the Northwest, it could be on a bench under a willow tree at Spokane's Riverfront Park, a wildflower trail in Mount Rainier, an old family cabin on a high mountain lake, or a rock ledge overlooking Oregon's wild Pacific coastline. What we find in common in such places is a quieting of our worries, a sense of being ourselves, a perspective.

Such places are often also indoors, the hearth places and people that nourished us and abide in memory long after we've left. The scent of cinnamon might trigger memories of your family at a kitchen table where laughter and conversation gave a sense of belonging; or hearing a saxophone solo brings flashbacks of the band room in junior high where the

music teacher built your confidence as a musician; or watching a basketball game reminds you of peer acceptance as your talents grew while playing on a high school team.

Because Krista Colleagues have been nominated as leaders, we are grateful for the families, communities, and heart places that have previously nurtured their development. It takes a certain amount of confidence and courage to choose to volunteer, including a belief that your commitment and talents will contribute to a community, and the humility to know you will have much to learn alongside others.

Yet as they emerge from deep sustained engagement in their service assignment, many Colleagues find that the suffering they witnessed can be almost overwhelming and often discouraging. Our hope is the genuine friendships with peers that they begin at the Hearth, the times of reflection on their service journey, and the tangible support of an intergenerational faith community expand their confidence and courage to continue living lives of engagement.

JOE MARTINEZ

"What I learned as a Krista Colleague totally changed my concept of service," says Joe Martinez. "I use the skills and insights gained from the IDI (intercultural inventory) and on 'accompanying others' every day." After graduating from the University of Washington, and his service with AmeriCorps, he became an International Labor Advocate with United Farm Workers as their Mexican Program Director.

For three years, he interviewed hundreds of Mexicans trying to come to America on H-2A bilateral agreements. "So many faced rampant corruption and even slavery from criminal elements and sex traffickers."

Fluent in Spanish, English, and Russian, what Joe observed led him to form his own company, CIERTO, with the ambitious goal of creating a safe, transparent, international workforce. His innovative pilot projects, in collaboration with the Howard G. Buffett Foundation, are expanding each year as he works closely to accompany all the stakeholders who provide America's fruits and vegetables. "To be truly effective in creating change, it's important to hear and understand the perspective of growers, the supply chain executives (such as Costco), as well as the farmworkers." In 2018, Joe traveled to Italy to receive an award from the United Nations Department of International Farm Workers to CIERTO for its model program, the first ever given to a North American. ✑

We saw how important such support proved to be for Krista's own faith journey in her twenties. She had been nurtured by many places of the heart, but was particularly influenced by participating in an environmental Young Leader's community in her twenties. After a retreat in the beauty of the Colorado mountains, the friendships with inspiring people infused her with greater confidence and gave her a boldness in making life choices.

In her journal, she writes on August 18, 1995, "I think reflection may be truly important. I'm noticing I am more true to myself being in nature, feel more open, more sincere." Her prayer that week was for for more clarity on the best ways to use the strengths and gifts God had given her. She then writes, "Thank you God for this boost of peace, confidence, joy and friendship. These people motivate and stir up my passion for You and for others."

Krista's writings reinforced the Krista Foundation vision. We hope to encourage Colleagues' confidence that their contributions, ethically given, are very needed in our world. We also hope to enliven their sense of courage as they recognize they are not alone. They can access two-pronged support: God is with them, and a community is with them.

Ricky Ruiz remembers when he first walked into the Hearth community to meet his cohort class and didn't know a soul. "I was surprised how I immediately felt a sense of peace and relaxed. I felt at home." He was nominated to be a Krista Colleague for his exceptional leadership in Rockwood, a low-income, diverse, densely populated neighborhood in Gresham, Oregon. He carries a passion to help children in his community and his efforts led to the transformation of an abandoned 28,000-square-foot skating rink into a futsal field (a smaller soccer field). Here children could play their city version of this favorite sport.

RIGHT We plant for seasonal interest, like this tree with white blossoms in the spring and beautiful berries in the fall.

"This place brings 'hope' and a sense of 'place' in a world so displaced and full of people without hope."

~Nim Hong

Later, it was attending a Debriefing retreat that cemented Ricky's understanding and confidence in how he could continue to help his neighborhood where he grew up. "My whole mindset changed after the weekend retreat. Being with other Colleagues reinforced my vision for serving. It wasn't about me, but about my desire for children in my impoverished neighborhood where I grew up. They deserved opportunities and a voice. We had built two fields by securing grants and partnership with the Portland Timbers Fields for All program. That's all I could imagine."

As he looks back on the weekend's influence in "recharging my batteries," he laughs at the impact of his renewed determination and ambition. "We've now built seven fields and are about to complete our eighth." He's also built lasting friendships with other Colleagues, an ongoing community of support.

During these transition years, perspective can be very useful. When Krista Colleagues gather for Debriefing Retreats, our staff sometimes shares a Passover poem by Alla Renee Bozarth to give context to the key importance of faithfulness in one's life journey. Bozarth shares an understanding that we are part of something larger than our individual story. Together, we are part of a larger God story in all its wonder and mystery. On the importance of reflection and storytelling within community, she writes, "Stories you tell one another around your fires in the dark will make you strong and wise."

BELOW The Northwest Room includes art from regional artists and beautiful views into the Asian gardens, Mount Spokane, and the Latin American courtyard.

NORTHWEST ROOM

Early morning sun pours into our upstairs corner room with windows overlooking the Asian garden and Latin American patio. We wanted to honor the culture of this region of the United States, so we created this Northwest Room. More like a guest room in a bed and breakfast inn, an Oregon woodworker crafted a queen bed and night stand with hand-rubbed finishes of western maple. A quilt with a pioneer design, regional water color art and prints, plus an antique pine Scandinavian armoire give a simple freshness to the room. An extra trundle bed can accommodate two more guests or families with children. One guest wrote,

> So much care, attention, time invested in this lovely place...reminds us of those lovely lines from "The Lake Isle of Innisfree" by W.B. Yeats.
>
> "I can find some peace there, For peace comes dropping slow..."

ROCKS AND TREES

If trees offer a sense of rootedness, the placement of large rocks, basalt rockeries, stepping stones to the Hearth, smooth rounded rocks in the ponds, and the stone root cellar give a sense of permanence and heft. They are staying put in a mobile world. Built on a basalt ledge, the land has so much stone that we benefit from earlier owners who utilized these to build long rockeries up the driveway, a three-tiered rock garden going up the hill to the barn, and other rockeries throughout to delineate pathways and hillsides. When an excavator came to replace a broken-down wooden staircase that connected our home to the Hearth, he used large bronze rock slabs for a winding staircase. So integrated into the hillside, it felt like an artist had designed the space.

JALEESA TRAPP

When Jaleesa Trapp volunteered with middle school girls in Tacoma's after-school Computer Clubhouse founded by Massachusetts Institute of Technology (MIT) Media Lab, she carried memories of her own powerful experiences there beginning in seventh grade. She discovered a passion and talent learning how to code, work on video games, and do graphic design. While a teenager, she twice attended the International Teen Summit in Boston.

This ultimately led to an undergraduate engineering degree at the University of Washington in human-computer interactions. She often found herself as the only person of color in the classroom and the only woman. "But I had confidence in the knowledge I'd learned from my years in the Computer Clubhouse. This motivated my return to Tacoma's Computer Clubhouse to open STEM fields to other young girls." She'd also made deep connections at the Hearth with other Colleagues, especially those serving in Tacoma. "I now felt like part of a village. We helped each other a lot!"

Presently a graduate student in MIT's Media Arts and Science program, she finds it fascinating understanding how people learn, especially with technology. At present, she's also engaged in redesigning the Teen Summit so youth can have more impact back in their communities. "To develop leaders, we say that when you learn something, it's your job to teach at least two other people the same thing." ❧

Looking up from chairs around the Latin American patio, or a hammock in the Asian garden, or out a window in the Hearth, it almost seems like the Hearth and gardens are cradled by the surrounding strength of towering trees. Many grew here long before we arrived, and their presence drew us to this land. "We couldn't live long enough to grow trees of this magnitude," I remember telling Jim when considering this property. We first saw it in May and he also felt drawn to the many scented honeysuckles, lilacs, grape arbors, and tall honey locust trees.

The 1940s house and barn clearly needed significant attention, but the setting carved into a hillside ledge, surrounded by magnificent spruce and native Ponderosa pines, was so distinctive and inviting.

The Ponderosa pines were first documented in America in 1826, actually near our Eastern Washington town of Spokane. Called a Ponderosa for its heavy wood, the massive erect evergreens, with their rusty orange bark etched with charcoal crevices, can adapt to many variable habitats.

Most of our acreage is an undeveloped hillside where large cottonwoods, fed by hidden springs, live near dozens of mock orange bushes. When their fragrant white flowers bloom, with nectar that draws butterflies, their beauty lights the terrain each spring.

Over the years, we have enhanced the gardens with ornamental trees that add immense seasonal interest. A Sunset maple and various species of Japanese maples and an American sweetgum tree, sumac, and witch hazel set the gardens ablaze in the fall with shimmering hues of amber, red, bronze, and green.

"This weekend was instrumental in me finding hope in the midst of hardship and despair. It provided accompaniment, love, and concrete tools for resilience and empowered me to grow 'strong and wise' through my time of service. My heart has learned the ability to hold ambiguity gently and engage in a *JOY DANCE* in all situations."

~Misch Kange, Krista Colleague
   serving in South Africa

RICHARD KELLEY

A 2011 Colleague, Richard moved to South Africa to Mamelodi, a township outside Pretoria. Through service in African Enterprise, Richard was able to build the Mamelodi Initative providing educational opportunity for youth. He now travels twice a year to South Africa to provide ongoing support for this non-profit.

A graduate of Harvard University, after completing his service experience, he attended Georgetown Law School and practiced law for a non-profit assisting women affected by domestic violence, and for immigration issues. He has recently joined DLA Piper in Washington D.C., one of the largest global law firms, to focus on litigation. "In a bigger law firm, one has the possibility of major impact on policy that can affect the lives of so many."

At his first Debriefing Retreat, he found the focus on marrying faith and intercultural competence transformative. "I also appreciated the recognition and permission for ambiguity in life." Now a board member of the Krista Foundation, he enjoys his visits back to the Hearth. "It has been one of my favorite places in the world to go because it is so peaceful. It allows me to slow down and be calm with others, a rarity in my life."

In spring, after Spokane's long bleak winters, when the large maple trees burst forth with their young lime green leaves, it's a long-anticipated visual pleasure. Then, there's a gentle profusion of trees beginning to bloom. The pink and white flowering dogwoods, a Japanese Kwanzan cherry tree, pink tulip trees, and Laburnum golden chain, choke-cherry, and fruit trees bud forth with their delicate welcome to the coming summer. After seeing an unusual 100-year-old yellow "Elizabeth" magnolia in Boston, we returned home and planted one that now thrives. These trees, plus the year round evergreens, such as Alaska cedars and blue spruce, offer a mosaic where birds and squirrels make their nests. They reach high to capture the light energy and convert it into sugars by photosynthesis, and providing the food for the trees' growth and development.

They provide shade, give food, create nooks to pause, and textural wonder, freshen the air, remove carbon dioxide, and live into their own distinctive purpose. Of course, they also need care, whether pruning, feeding, or transplanting. They can create a temporary deluge of leaves or blossoms that need raking as they shed in the fall and spring. But I rather like the 13th century Persian poet Rumi's perspective, "Hear blessings dropping their blossoms around you."

Some have cracked and fallen in the storms and needed to be removed, a recognition of impermanence that prevails. Yet, even then, they continue to give. Whether for split rail fences, wood frames for people's homes, or firewood for hearths, stumps for sitting, or nurse logs that feed insect life for centuries,

If the trees were stripped from the land, we would feel a barenness from beauty. It's impossible to imagine how bereft we would be without their gifts to the living world. They give a sense of strength to the land, knowing many have lived long before our presence and will continue beyond our time. ꙮ

Epilogue: Celebrating the Seasons

*"To every thing there is a season,
and a time to every purpose under the heaven...
a time to weep and a time to laugh;
a time to mourn and a time to dance.*

~Ecclesiastes 3, KJV

Celebrating the Season

Epilogue

The Hearth and gardens began in a season of mourning, a time when our shattered hearts needed a tangible way to express the love we carried for our daughter Krista. For family and friends who grieved her loss deeply, it also gave a focus for healing. They joined us by designing stained glass windows, building shoe racks, bringing artisan rugs from Latin America, refinishing furniture, planting trees and flowers, and cooking meals for all who helped. Each creative action added to the joy as this retreat space developed.

In the following years, especially as the gardens flourished, it not only became an illuminating place of healing for our extended family and friends, but radiated out to the many guests who found this hillside retreat offered a pause, a visual place of peace, refreshment and renewal.

As we reread the Blessings prayed for almost twenty years ago, and then reread guestbook comments, we realized how much such spaces are needed in our fast paced, stress-inducing world. Wherever in their personal journey a guest arrives, we hope that the Hearth plants life-affirming seeds. Everyone carries some fragments of pain, loss, or disappointment, and often people are doing their best to live with resilience and strength in a complex world. Year after year, season after season, the Hearth and gardens give a visual reminder of the truth that, in time, even the deepest mourning can turn into a joy dance of celebration.

Although it offers a centering home for some of our events, the Hearth and gardens are only one part of the far larger Krista Foundation for Global Citizenship. The expansive program originating from our Seattle office happens all year long in many different places. There are now over 316 Krista Colleagues that have served in over 60 countries and 55 American cities. National recognition of our innovative Krista Colleague program,

BELOW A Christmas party with neighborhood children, always a favorite time.

"The Hearth has been a place of healing for my soul, 'book ending' if you will, the death of Cameron. A safe haven in March of 2002, a place to share grief, sorrow, tears, joy, and laughter with other moms. Blessings for sharing this journey with me."

~Jan Skaggs

ABOVE (left) We found this ancient beloved Celtic prayer in a large leather reproduction that graces the main floor in the Hearth, the same quote on our original thank you notes to all who came alongside us in our sorrow.

Debriefing Retreats, and service-ethics preparation has led to the Krista Foundation providing consulting and training to other young adult service organizations throughout the country. This has been a gratifying by-product of our work.

Wherever hospitality shines, where all persons are welcomed, accepted and loved, where food, drink, music, and conversation flourish, these are hearth places. Jim and I have had the pleasure of visiting some of our Krista Colleagues once they settle into their post-assignment lives. We are delighted to see ways they are creating their own hearth spaces wherever they live. We've visited a Colleague who offered a safe drop-in home in a gang neighborhood in Hilltop Tacoma; we've enjoyed Bolivian empanadas in a suburban cul-de-sac in greater Seattle; we've feasted on homemade bread on a Sunday afternoon in a tiny graduate school apartment in Princeton; and we've celebrated a graduation picnic in a rental on a Native American reservation. Many Colleagues carry memories of the immense generosity they encountered from citizens they served alongside in poor neighborhoods or villages. They learned it really doesn't matter where one creates a hearth place as long as a spirit of open hearts comes within open doors.

At the heart of all celebrations is thanksgiving. We gather in thankfulness for the breath of life when a baby is born, for the goodness of friendships and family to mark birthdays and anniversaries, for the courage and commitment to love at weddings, for challenges met at graduations, and for remembrances of a beloved person at Memorial gatherings. Most often these are communal times, where friends and family come together and build memories.

At the Hearth, such celebrations happen often. Our very first was the picnic with friends where we walked the footprint of the future Hearth and read our Blessings together. Most recently, over 100

ABOVE Forget-me-nots and lilies bloom each spring near Krista's memorial garden.

came to join with us in a garden party in gratitude for 50 years of marriage. Many of these same guests came alongside us in sorrow many years ago as we planted a Weeping Cherry in a memorial garden to remember and celebrate the life of Krista. Celebrations for Cinco de Mayo, cousins' reunions, wedding showers, Christmas neighborhood parties, music concerts, and book launches are among the many events. Such celebrations give everyone an opportunity to pause, to recognize the important people and events in our lives, even to appreciate how feasts of food, music, dance, and flowers add festive creativity to ordinary days.

Such major milestones are important.

However, living with an appreciation of the sheer wonders within the smaller moments of daily life also offers a way of being that feeds the soul. These might be quiet individual times of awareness that lead to an inner celebration of gratitude. This happens most often for Jim and me as we move through the seasons in the gardens. Plants need tending. They require the nourishment of quality

soil and nutrients, pruning, protection from harmful insects, and transplanting when they fail to thrive. Still, loss happens. Some plants get diseased and die, like our treasured Frost Peach tree that once produced the rare treat of sun-ripened peaches on a summer day. But, with care, others show resilience and rebound.

In exchange for this garden caretaking, we are offered daily glimpses of wonder. The snow on the pink cones of a healthy Korean pine, the vibrancy of a tender spring salad with Baby's Leaf spinach, Cherry Belle radishes, and Little Finger carrots that were tiny seeds weeks earlier, the slender blue and lavender Siberian iris that begin with a dull brown tuber, the blue eggs in a common robin's nest, or the annual return of the honeybees when the pink cherry tree blooms—wonders abound! If we are attentive, each of these moments open our lives to the beauty and rhythms that exist in the world. We don't need to wait for milestone events.

We just need space in our souls to live with daily thanksgiving. ✇

Notes

Mutual Invitation Process: Chapter IV
The Wolf Shall Dwell with the Lamb, Dr. Eric H.F. Law

After introducing the process, the leader, or a designated person, will share first. After that person has spoken, they invite another to share. After the next person has spoken, that person is given the privilege to invite another to share. Recognizing that some people may not be ready or want to share when asked, they have three options:

1. They can share. Then invite someone after you.

2. If someone is not ready to share yet, they can say "I pass for now," and they will be invited again later on. They also invite the next person.

3. If someone doesn't want to say anything at all, they simply say "pass" and proceed to invite another to share. The group will do this until everyone has been invited.

The Daily Examen

Many variables of this St. Ignatius practice have emerged over the centuries, but most include five similar key elements.

1. Stillness: Recall God's Presence. Become aware of God's presence and ask God for light and the ability to look at oneself through God's eyes. Give thanks for God's great love for you.

2. Give Thanks: Reviewing the day with gratitude. Consciously recall all the gifts of God in your life. Pay attention to the small things, whether the smile of a neighbor child or the hot water and electricity in your day.

3. Pay attention to your experiences. Recall specific moments and your feelings at the time. What made you happy? What made you stressed? What confused you? What helped you be more loving?

4. Reflect on what you did, said, or thought in those instances. Were you drawing closer to God (times of consolation) or further away (times of desolation).

5. Look toward tomorrow. Ask how you might collaborate more effectively with God's plan. Be specific.

Afterword

Venturing and Abiding

It has been said that a good life is formed in the alchemy of both venturing and abiding. This deep rhythmic motion can evolve into yet larger significance during the twenty-something years, when we begin to emerge into full adulthood. As we push off from our familiar home places, we are ripe for exploring new landscapes both external and internal. We are poised for adventures both promising and perilous, as we reach toward taking full responsibility for how we think, act, and believe in a dramatically changing world.

The development of our capacity for critical thought (the ability to step outside our own thinking and wonder, "Why do I think that way?") and our capacity for connective thought (the ability to "connect the dots" and recognize that everything is connected to everything else) gives us new powers. These new powers can carry us into a more profound recognition of the suffering and wonder of our world, and they can plunge us into paralyzing doubt and the specter of meaninglessness. It is also possible to glide through these years on the surface of things and miss a deeper calling into a life that can make a meaningful difference for both self and others.

Thus the twenty-something years harbor a distinctive mix of promise and vulnerability. And the achievement of a meaningful adulthood, therefore, typically requires access to mentoring environments that young adults need and deserve. Mentoring environments "see" the unique promise of an emerging adult life, provide support and challenge, and inspire worthy dreams.

The Krista Foundation has become a mentoring environment with a special genius for honoring the alchemy of venturing and abiding of the twenty-something years. The Foundation provides practical support for young adults who *venture* into serving in a wide variety of projects, and it also has created places of pause, hospitality, and inspiration where young adults discover the value of *abiding*.

The Hearth is such a space—a place for the soul to rest, learn, heal, and grow. A small scruffy barn was transformed into a remarkable guesthouse, a place of warmth, welcome, belonging, and the kind of pause in which the soul is nourished.

The Hearth provides a fresh initiation into the practices of abiding: Time alone in a quiet "room of one's own," or in the garden, or at the fireplace, to reflect, journal, meditate, pray, or otherwise take in, absorb, digest, examine, laugh, weep, reconsider, and discover a more adequate understanding of self, world—and "God."

The Hearth also provides time with others who are venturing, and who similarly are discovering the need for home places that evoke *staying* as well as *moving*. The alchemy of hearth and table (reflective conversation over food shared in common) yields companionship in the midst of venturing, strengthening the formation of citizenship and leadership—lives prepared to make a difference in world of suffering and wonder.

–Sharon Daloz Parks

Acknowledgments

From the first evening, when friends came for a picnic and we walked the future perimeter to offer our prayers of "Blessings for the Hearth," Jim and I have known this vision thrives because of the community of support surrounding us. Whether Krista Colleagues, artisans, builders, gardeners, or painters, our guests' stories give vibrant life to our efforts to create a living legacy for Krista, including this *Soul Space* book. Though far too many to name, there are some that brought particular expertise and commitment to having this story emerge.

Judi Bergen of Toronto gave hours and hours to reading of drafts, critiquing, and offering organizational recommendations that proved immensely helpful as I sifted through 18 years of experiences, guest book quotes, and Krista Colleague stories. As I imagined introducing others to stories within the Hearth and gardens, I knew this needed to be a visual book. I'm so grateful for my wise book consultant and friend Roy Carlisle who introduced me to the exceptionally talented Graphic Artist Barbara Genetin. For months Barbara and I worked long distance online, and each time her sample pages came in, her sensitivity, creativity, and talent thrilled me. My great pleasure was finally working alongside her in California and seeing how she exudes such expertise and beauty in her art and her spirit. A very talented copy editor, Cecilia Santini, added her essential expert eye to *Soul Space*.

The photographs that have been collected through the years begin with Krista's days in Bolivia, and unfortunately, I do not know the photographers for many of the photos. Most of the early Bolivian pictures came from Krista's husband, Aaron Ausland. Within the Krista Foundation, Tom Norwood and Diakonda Gurning provided many of the candid shots from the Colleague events at the Hearth. Megan Hammon surprised me with the gift of time with Robin Brazill, a professional Spokane photographer who added some of the interior pictures. A budding high school photographer, Henry Moe, brought his original eye both to interior and garden scenes, and Marla Hyder sent us the dismantling of the barn scene. Barbara Safranek, a landscape designer, introduced us to talented plant photographer Jerry Pavia who asked to use our land for his garden portfolio. Jim and I have taken many of the rest, especially as we find ourselves thrilled with some daily wonder we've seen in the garden, whether a praying mantis on a dahlia, the tiger swallowtail butterflies flitting through the flowers, or the unfurling of a spring fern leaf.

We live with thanksgiving for all.

About the Author

Linda Lawrence Hunt, co-founder of the Krista Foundation for Global Citizenship, taught at Whitworth University as director of the Writing Program and helped establish their strong Service-Learning program. A two-time cancer survivor, she enjoys speaking across America on living with boldness, resilience, and hope in challenging times. She is author of several books, including the award-winning *Bold Spirit: Helga Estby's Forgotten Walk Across Victorian America* and *Pilgrimage through Loss: Pathways to Strength and Renewal after the Death of a Child*. A University of Washington graduate, her Ph.D. in Leadership Studies from Gonzaga University provided excellent background as the Foundation designed initial programs to honor her and Jim's daughter Krista's life. She finds daily wonder in the gardens around their home and the Hearth, a healing place where creativity and joy abounds.

Author Website: www.lindalawrencehunt.com